Gypsy Guitar

GYPSY GUITAR

One Hundred Poems of Romance and Betrayal

David McFadden

Talonbooks • Vancouver • 1987

published with the assistance of the Canada Council

Talonbooks
201/1019 East Cordova Street
Vancouver, B.C. V6A 1M8
Canada

Typeset in Goudy Oldstyle Condensed by Pièce de Résistance.
Printed and bound in Canada by Hignell Printing Ltd.

First printing: October 1987.

Canadian Cataloguing in Publication Data

McFadden, David, 1940-
   Gypsy guitar

   Poems.
   ISBN 0-88922-250-9

   I. Title.
PS8525.F32G9 1987   C811'.54   C87-091456-1

For the Venerable Ryokan, who in spite of his solitude
and his certificate of enlightenment from the local Buddhist temple
still wrote disgraceful haiku with the wrong number of syllables
and still entertained himself with fantasies
of love and longing, ravishment and revenge.

And it breaks my heart altogether to see
a grim husband with a lovely wife....
The Monk of Montaudon

Contents

1. Il Vecchio Is Our Love
2. Night Bus to Montreal
3. Love's Like Milk
4. Love's Two Hemispheres
5. A Visit to the Zoo
6. Tortured by Kahlil Gibran
7. Elephants
8. Afternoon Bus to Toronto
9. Light and Laughter
10. La Traviata
11. Spring in Toronto
12. Shantideva
13. The Worst of People
14. The CN Tower
15. My Grandmother Learns to Drive
16. Blazing Nirvana
17. The Inchworm
18. Blue Irises
19. Terrible Storm on Lake Erie
20. If I Were a Buddhist
21. Lion in the Road
22. The Moons of Jupiter
23. Separation Anxiety
24. Dogs That Never Disappear
25. Airpipe to the Surface
26. Transparencies
27. Windsurfers
28. Late Afternoon Rainfall
29. Midsummer Garden Party
30. God's Way of Remaining Anonymous
31. The Snake
32. Gossip
33. Nightmares
34. The Road to Thunder Bay
35. Beauty and Remoteness
36. In the Buffalo Airport
37. The Sea Captain
38. Over the Rainbow
39. How to Be Your Own Butcher
40. Christian Wildflowers
41. Geneva Violets

42. Invisibility
43. My Own True Nature
44. Death Beds
45. Richard II
46. Nipples
47. The Robe of Your Intelligence
48. Beer and Pizza
49. Yoko Ono
50. God Save the Queen!
51. Zen
52. Caucasian Shower
53. Ocean of Sadness
54. The Sacrifice of Desire
55. Woman Descending from a Train
56. My Secret Ambition
57. Accordion Solo
58. The Two of Cups
59. Trying to Figure It Out
60. My Old Diaries
61. Peace
62. Cadillac Moon
63. An Artist's Prayer
64. The Spirit of Toronto
65. Heading towards Buchenwald
66. Monkey on My Back
67. The Universal Ecstasy of Things
68. Jellyfish of Light
69. Elephants on Television
70. Have a Nice Day
71. Star
72. Conversation with a Small Herd of Cattle
73. Hell
74. Green
75. Membrane of Bliss
76. My Chocolate Maserati
77. Walter's Moustache
78. Another Plate of Fudge
79. My Brother's Poetry
80. The Taming of the Shark
81. Consciousness
82. Perceptual Error
83. Crime Prevention Measures
84. Sailing in Perfect Space
85. Early Autumn
86. Listen to the Angels
87. Baby Birds
88. The Piano Player
89. That Great Diamond Ring in the Sky
90. How to Quit Smoking
91. The Poetry of Our Age
92. A Date with Margaret Hollingsworth
93. The Lock on Basho's Gate
94. The Nosferatu Syndrome
95. Christmas Eve at the Movies
96. Hummingbirds at Hell's Gate
97. The Women in My Life
98. A Home Run Is a Glorious Thing
99. Proust
100. Dead Hippopotamus

Preface

It's as if I were to become (belatedly) interested in the notion of reason over passion in the sense of dynamic spiritual tension, of the battle between St. George and the Dragon. This is a battle with no beginning. When we are young we begin to notice it and it is as if it were always there. It is foolish to think the battle can ever be won by either side, and maybe the battle is not a battle at all. To mutilate a line of Blake: Reason is in love with the forces of passion. In late childhood, when we notice we are no longer so afraid of the dark, we become sad. In early childhood we thought those birds were fighting but they were really mating.

It's as if you went to Glastonbury, the place where Arthur and Guinevere are buried, where there are ancient oak trees and magical roses planted by Joseph of Arimathea, where there are people who believe that Jesus came there to study with the Druids before he started performing miracles, and a very nice man played his harp for you. You were embarrassed because you did not like his playing and could not give him the praise he was expecting, for there was no darkness in his music, he had convinced himself that he was the great hero who had slain the dragon. Later it came to you that any sentimental but sincere Gypsy Guitarist half-drunk and singing through his tears was more likely to make your hair stand on end than a host of heavenly harpists.

It's as if we were there together, two individual human beings among the mythical beasts, and I were asking you not to ask me how these poems came to be. I have no idea how she did it but it's as if an imaginary being, an "onlie begetter," suddenly created the necessity for their existence. Maybe the poems are about inspiration. About how an imaginary being—say the wife of the man who played the harp for instance—came into my life and suddenly I knew I could calm storms and make comets appear. About angels who know me better than does my mother. About my mother. About all the mothers whose babies will starve. About a thought it might be nice to have some day. About someone who can't stand Toronto. About someone whose nervous system for one moment I thought was the other half of my own. About someone I thought might be able to help me in my hobby of creating miniature alternate universes. About someone with whom I had an inexplicable feeling I could give birth to something that had some kind of divine destiny. About someone who has learned not to take poets seriously ("You sentimental schmuck!" or "I could never be married to a poet!"). About someone who lived and died without ever having had the pleasure of being acquainted with me. About someone who hasn't learned I'm not really what you'd call a real poet. And, most embarrassing of all, about someone who, before these bloated, overblown sonnets (as I sometimes think of them) were written, was exploited for their sake, and to whom I hereby offer apologies.

It's as if over the past couple of years I've been possessed of a simple faith that all of this commotion has some kind of ultimate meaning, that I have written these poems is in some way a good thing, and that you are about to read them, or some of them, is too.

It's as if I must plead for purity and warmth of heart with those who may be picking up this book for the first time. To read a book of poetry is to form a bond with the writer. A writer whose poems are live leg-traps through the real prey is the writer himself.

It's as if I can get away with this because in my heart I know we're all one. But then again, what if everyone started saying that? Maybe they do. I'm sure they do. Or else how could I have possibly said it?

It's as if in these poems the I is not I and the you is not you. That's simple enough, but in addition the I and the you are one.

It's as if as a reader you were invited to read these poems as if they were your own, as if you were the you and I were the I, or as if you were the I and I were the you, or as if both you and I were the you and the I at the same time.

At any rate, it's just you and me, reader.

Naked (spiritually) in each other's (spiritual) arms.

For after all we've known each other (spiritually) for ever.

David McFadden

1. Il Vecchio Is Our Love

When your husband finds out he'll be furious but so far we've escaped
detection. We're a pair of littermates and when we're together we're
alert and quiet. "Tell the bishops I'm not doing this for the Church,
I'm doing it for Italy," said the printer Luigi Brizi in 1943 when he
finally agreed (after deep deliberation) to the priest's request to print
hundreds of fake identity cards for the Jews hiding in the San Quilico
convent in Assisi. As for us, we're not doing it for ourselves but for
the world, it's our civic duty to be together, to contribute all we can
to the world's dwindling supplies of felicity. For love makes heroes
of us all but love is the true hero. It finds us and brings us sweetly
to life. I fantasize that under the most unspeakable tortures I would
steadfastly refuse to reveal your identity. And if we're caught and
hanged we'll die smiling like that famous photo we were talking about
an hour before it appeared on the TV screen. Two Polish kids who'd
been taking pot shots at the Germans. The girl had been hanged, you
could see her smiling, dead. The boy, looking at her, smiling, the
noose being placed over his head. Better world to come. At thirty-two
Gino Battaglia was already called Il Vecchio ("The Old Bozo") because
he'd lost his title as champion of all Italy to someone ten years younger.
It was Il Vecchio who stuffed the photos and papers down the frame
of his bicycle and rode again and again between San Quilico and
Luigi's shop in San Damiano, and each time he did he passed a series
of German checkpoints. The Germans laughed as he rode by, east with
the photos, west with the cards, they thought he was in training,
desperate to win his title back. And he was too, and he did win it
back after the war. In fact he went on to win the Tour de France.

I know you'll forgive my disdain for poetic subtlety if I state that
I am those fake identity cards, you are that Italian racing bike, your
husband is one of those German sentries, the tall one with the grim
smile, anxious to know your racial origin, and Il Vecchio is our love.

After Alexander Ramati's *The Assisi Underground.*

2. Night Bus to Montreal

With a copy of Nagatsuka's *I Was a Kamikaze* on my lap
(for courage) I dozed and dreamt of a curious volcanic crater,
innocent on the earth, filled with a chalky fluid that tasted
like flat club soda, with an opening that came up to my chest.
I dove in and swam with furious grace through a subterranean
tunnel illuminated with subtle colours that never existed and I
wondered if I'd ever breathe again until I woke with a gasp.
The bus had stopped in a small town, half a moon in the sky.
A man was half-trying to fix his motorcycle on the sidewalk
under a lamp. A tall man with his arm half-around a short woman
crossed the street towards the man trying to fix his motorcycle
and they walked past him without saying hello. The first man lit
a cigarette, tried to start his motorcycle one last time, failed,
then hopped on and coasted quietly down the hill and out of sight.

The moon kept shining. The driver started the bus first try and we
headed back out to the expressway. I dozed again and dreamed
of an old man with bad breath who came up to me in a bookstore
and said that pouring hot water into a mixture of powdered mint,
ginger and carob made a delicious nightcap. Add honey to taste.
He said he was a government nutritional researcher (retired) and
suggested I give up eating chocolate forever. The next day, in the
humour section (I needed a laugh) of a Westmount bookstore an old
man came up as if he'd known me in previous lives, gave me a small
whiff of bad breath, and immediately started telling me how to make
a delicious nightcap. And as he left he said it'd improve my dreams.

3. Love's Like Milk

You were right, your cat knows his own name. He's asleep right now,
but earlier he proved it to my hard-nosed satisfaction. He also knows
about us! The only one who does! I stuck your copy of the Eaton's
catalogue in the window to stop it from banging in the wind. I like it
here. Maybe I should feel like one of Penelope's suitors but I don't.
Well, maybe I do, but not as I imagine one of Penelope's suitors
feeling, if you see the difference. It's an entirely different story.
I want my life to be as simple as our mutual attraction is simple.
Next year when you-know-who returns even that'll be simple.
I ask myself, sitting here silent as the cat, what should I do: a car
passes by the house the wrong way and a passionately concerned
pedestrian hollers: "One way!" And Zasep the Tibetan lama, when I
said love is like milk, it starts sweet and ends sour, said that's often
the case but not always, his opinion based on numerous discussions
with people who hadn't spent their lives in total celibacy, and when
I asked him if he ever had sexual dreams he said oh yes and he told of
dreaming he was in bed with a young woman and there was another
lama lying on her other side. He said it was strange and she shone
like a prehistoric Tibetan goddess. Two lamas in silent adoration.

Since I arrived someone has painted a happy face on the chimney
of the house across the street and it stares in at us like a household
god, the historic kind who likes to spy on neighbours and is gifted
with special knowledge of the past and present but alas is incapable
of telling the future. At times he seems pleased, at times mocking.
That's always the case, says Zasep: when you're actively searching
for a lover the one you find turns out to be unsuitable, but when you
sit quietly at home angels, one after the other, knock at your door.

4. Love's Two Hemispheres

I'm a true Canadian but it's not my fault if I can't stand Canadian beer
and cigarettes, much prefer American, and as for our literature and wine,
let's be honest one must choose carefully. If I'd been born in 1920
I'd have fought and probably died in France or Italy, but I was born in
1940 and remain untouched (except merely in my heart and soul)
by Buchenvald, Hiroshima, Dresden, Vietnam or Beirut. And so I've
survived into the eighties and am witnessing on behalf of God and all
the angels the scenario jokingly predicted by D. H. Lawrence in 1916:
"The people of the world divided into two halves, and each half decided
it was perfect and right, the other half was wrong and must be destroyed."

This afternoon, with the two hemispheres busy building bombs bigger
than the blasted biosphere without asking what you and I think about it all,
we lay, as if waiting for the destruction to come, like little lions
in each other's warm and sunny arms on the grassy, warm and sunny spit
at Saint-Jean-sur-Richelieu, prosperous Québécois passing in pretty
yachts and politely ignoring our lovely semi-naked affections. We
were two hemispheres, and I touched you and told you that you were
perfect and full of wonders, and you did and said the same, and so
we became transformed, and refused to believe we'd ever be destroyed
because we were not only ourselves but everyone and everything.

5. A Visit to the Zoo

Thirty minutes until feeding time in the cathouse at the Granby
Zoo, and the lions, tigers, pumas, panthers and other assorted
passionate, beautiful and mindless carnivores explode and explode
again with wild and furious insanity. In the wild they'd be consuming
all this intensity in the hunt. Here the bars and the sliding doors of
inch-thick glass are preserving them from the extinction they'd
face in the wild. But they don't know that. How amazing! Such enforced
patience! Such suffering! And above all, thick electrical clouds are
massing and it's about to rain huge globs of steaming adrenalin.
How removed this was, I thought, from Zasep the Tibetan lama, who is
totally celibate and always has been, and three times a week since
childhood has performed a special yoga technique for relieving sexual
tension, a technique involving violent exhalations and so on, and it
may be noted that he eats no meat and little of anything else. And how
far removed from us, grazing sweetly on each other's memories
since you appeared at my door like an angel with no luggage.

You should come back tomorrow, says the keeper, with his pails of raw
and steaming horsemeat from the horse farms of the Eastern Townships.
We don't feed them on Mondays and things really get tense.... Whew!
That's It, they think this might be Monday, they don't even have the
satisfaction of knowing for certain they're going to be fed on any
given day. Cats can't count to seven. In the air is no love, there is only
passionate hunger, and not the passionate hunger that can sometimes
be mistaken for love. And even us, we argue mildly about the weather.
And about whether or not to leave immediately. And I wonder if I'm
fooling myself when I think I understand what's in your heart and mind.

6. Tortured by Kahlil Gibran

The holy poets of antiquity tell us the foolish take the path
of pleasure, the wise the path of joy, but I must be the most
foolish of all for I continually try to take both simultaneously
and the amount of pleasure and joy I experience is almost nil.
At least I have the wisdom to reject wisdom as I offer myself
to the flames of hell as if it were a suntan parlour, a few
blistering moments at a time, amusing myself and doing my best
to amuse my friends, particularly you. I really do believe in
happiness, but it seems to be a genetic thing, like a cleft palate.
I cower in heaven gathering strength to stick my toe in hell,
and just before dawn I glanced out and was startled to see
the catalpa tree in front of my house seemed to have grown a
perfectly round, luminous leaf, but I soon realized I was merely
looking at the full moon shining through leafless branches.
A few minutes later I looked out again and was startled to see
on the crest of the hill to the south of the town a huge luminous
observatory, as if spacemen had landed and built it overnight.
But I looked again and realized it was again only the full moon,
and as I sat there watching it moved along the crest of the hill
and as it dipped towards the western horizon the hill dipped too.

And in the silence shortly after dawn I heard a slight rustling in
the garden and thought someone was digging up my bulbs, but when I
peeked out ready to pounce it was only a robin turning over leaves
for worms. And when I finally got to sleep I dreamt of a flower the
size of hell and as I dreamt it slowly opened like a subterranean vagina
and there in the centre I saw you being tortured by Kahlil Gibran.

7. Elephants

Knoxville, San Diego, Winnipeg, Buffalo, Granby, Toronto: a list
of zoos I've visited this year. And anyone could see the gorillas at the
Toronto Zoo were conscious, deliberate philosophers with no vocabulary,
sitting in the glass house pondering ambiguity, paradox and the absolutes.
At Granby the gorillas were of a decidedly lower class. I hope they don't
read this. Two big ones studiously ignored a tossed banana for several
tense minutes until finally the male broke down and flickered with
interest and the female leaped from her perch, pounced on the banana,
then ate it herself while the male tried to pretend he didn't care. And
an American eagle attacked his mate over a gerbil tossed in their cage.

Viciously too, all heaven in a rage. But when I held out a handful of
nuts to the bull elephant he took only half, then slowly backed up so his
mate could have the remainder. The eyes of these sad spiritual lovers in
leg chains checked to see if I understood and appreciated their little gesture
of kindness and love, and I felt I'd been blessed by the Pope. They knew
there was nothing I could do to free them, though when two doves were
presented to Pope John Paul II in Montreal he released them and they
didn't fly away, just sat there in transcendental splendour in the middle
of crowded Olympic Stadium, little haloes radiant. And people who live
in the vicinity of the Granby Zoo when you get to know them will shyly
confide in you that late at night after they turn off the television they lie
in bed listening to and feeling the earth and sky quivering and murmuring
with the mammoth heartbreaking hour-long orgasms of the elephants.

8. Afternoon Bus to Toronto

As we hold each other dull and loveless passersby sadly look away
under a blue sky at noon outside the Marigold Cafe in a city where
signs of affection must bear signs of official approval or be
restricted to the parks along the waterfront, behind the lilac
trees, under the quaking moon, and so on. Is it with joy or sadness
that everything we give away comes back to us, alone and awake?
In the bowling ball of the brain the third eye is the one at the rear,
looking in at the holy field in which the sport of the gods takes place:
an illuminated hockey rink smeared with blood and guts. We are not
each other but we're at one right now with ourselves and the world,
personal and global histories forming dim and unpredictable patterns.

My love for you forms patterns I immediately smash, your virginal
breasts have developed magnetic powers, my face becomes tanned
with pleasure, and we hold each other for a moment longer then part.
I don't imagine you looking back, I don't look back, and on the bus
I give my window seat to an elderly woman travelling with her
granddaughter and take a seat next to a woman who resembles you.
Before I can say what are you doing here I know it's impossible.
For a hundred miles I listen to the grandmother telling the little
girl over and over again what a kind gentleman I am for giving up
my seat and how nice it would be if more were like me, while I
quietly smash away at thin crusts of sadness as they form, platelets
of congealed desire, love's immensely wearying habit, and I become
quietly clever, inventive, courageous and consumed with solitude.

9. Light and Laughter

I knew your brother many years ago, but not that well, I said.
Did you know he was dead, she said, and I said no. He hanged
himself in a German jail, she said. He'd been touring Europe
with a woman he loved but who didn't love him, and when she
left him he became depressed, was thrown in jail for vagrancy,
and died without leaving a note. She and I were strangers, sitting
at the bar at Bemelman's where I'd gone to spend an hour or two
scanning a stack of unsolicited Harlequin Romance manuscripts.
She gave me a taste of her chicken and ginger fetuccini and I
gave her a taste of my drink. She said he was eleven years older
than she and had taught her many wonderful things about life.
Never give them the pleasure of seeing you cry, he taught her.
Losing hurts worse than winning feels good (he stole that one
from Joe Garagiola), and one can ultimately only betray oneself.
Don't build fortifications around your ego and if people abuse
your benevolence and Zen-like candour walk away from them.
She said his letters in retrospect had shown he'd become tired
of life, that he thought he'd experienced everything he could
and was anxious to go to his next incarnation. I said hey maybe
when you die you'll find him waiting there for you and she
smiled and told me about the rock band she was singing with.

We write all our own material, she said: songs about the poor
people of the world, the lonely, the wandering ones. We identify
with the sadness all around us, she said. Her face was thin and
serious, but she dressed and carried herself with a sense of joy,
laughed a lot, and radiated a certain invisible but tangible light.

10. La Traviata

I heard an elderly gentleman on the street say to his friend:
"The widow of Enrico Caruso told me my voice reminded her
strangely of her dead husband's." I'd just left the movie house
after seeing *La Traviata*, and I went home and found myself
brooding for hours about my childhood, when every experience
was charged with immense significance, when dreams and
waking life formed a wonderful mystery, and how up until a few
years ago every dream I dreamt was a dream of childhood. Extremes
of misery and joy in those far-off days were separated by a wink
and even while asleep I felt I was part of a band of angels and maybe
I was though adults of course knew nothing of this, they seemed
to be some kind of genetic robots and I knew that's what I was
going to become if I didn't watch out so I took a mighty vow never
to forget my sacred origins. And now I wish I hadn't taken that
vow, it'd be wonderful to be able to forget, it'd be such a treat
to become a robot like all the other robots instead of spending my
life writing sad endless poems far into the morning light, hoping
to retrieve what has haunted me through the years: unbroken bliss.

And so I dozed off and dreamt of a mermaid who led me through the
sea to an enchanted isle where in the golden sky dozens of pairs of
twin angels flashed their silvery twin-souls above the hills and
trees and little towns and the entire island was illuminated by their
radiance and I felt an absence of sorrow, a freedom from the dull
cares that rob us of bliss, and I found myself rising into the air,
and gradually the radiance of the angels became my own, and they
smiled and flashed their silvery twin-soul mirrors merrily at me
until I became conscious of being different, of having no twin, and
felt myself becoming heavy and floating softly back down to earth.

11. Spring in Toronto

I'm sitting on a bench on a warm Sunday evening watching the
colours changing and the sun setting behind office towers at Bloor
Street and Avenue Road and watching auto-crazed motorists zooming
past cyclists with an inch to spare and scattering little groups
of semi-somnambulistic pedestrians scrambling for sidewalk safety.
Someone is hanging by his thumbs from the roof of the Park Plaza
and the cops are trying to rescue him. A nutty old guy standing in the
road screaming about Hitler and Stalin has been knocked flying by a
van and the ambulance crew is trying to revive him. My friend Gwen
says she knows she's inventing all this and so am I but I'm not so
sure. If I were inventing all this I could merely by thinking about it
make the nutty old guy come alive again and run up the church steps
and start screaming anti-electric shock slogans and so I try but he
stays dead. As for the jumper, I will him to let go and fall into the
net the fire department is holding thirty storeys below but it looks
as if the cops have saved him. So it would appear that Gwen is wrong,
I'm not God. Maybe she is but I'm not. But then again maybe I'm inventing
myself not to be God while she's doing the opposite. Sure. Why not?
I will admit though that the universe is a strange place and nothing
I know or have ever been taught has any abiding truth. There are no
absolutes, even life and death are relative and can easily be transposed
by simple thought. When I say the body is a tomb for the soul I'm not
being pessimistic, but my friends hate to hear me say it. I tell Gwen
I want to save the world with my poetry, she says she saved the world
years ago. Everything's all right now. I remember a previous life when I
was a spring breeze rippling through a cherry orchard. Gwen can be God
if she wants, I just want to be a willing soldier in the swirl of cosmic
energy. Meanwhile I watch the people strolling by and I wonder about
my pathetic likes and dislikes. Why do I like the people I do and dislike
some? I dislike for instance men who wear suits with carefully knotted
ties on warm evenings. I dislike interracial couples who, as they pass,
look at you as if they expect you to disapprove. I dislike the fashions
of the young in general, and amorous couples who seem only to be
pretending to be comfortable with each other. I love the solitary
strollers who talk to themselves, reliving dramatic and traumatic
events of their lives and cursing aloud in the intensity of their
persistent somnambulism. I dislike bums who ask you for a quarter
and when you give them one ask for a dollar. I love nice old people
in their Sunday best just in from the suburbs, young slobbering
wasted bucks in their wheelchairs out on the make (who could
resist them?), unselfconscious old guys covered in dirt who poke
through the garbage bins looking for butts and empty bottles (and
if only for them at least I'm glad that spring is here again at last).

I find myself disliking pipesmokers whose pipes are too large for their
faces, but most of all I dislike the fact that you're not here with me.

After the fatuously arrogant Monk of Montaudon, whose *enuegs*, poems of annoyance and
vexation, were famous in thirteenth-century France and Spain.

12. Shantideva

Every day I try to do something that would make my mother proud of me if she knew about it. God, what's this guy going to say next? Oh, life is so embarrassing. I am only as innocent as you are. Never thought of that, didya? You know how much I smoke and what a hyena I am at the table. Well, when you were a kid did you sometimes think your mother could read your mind? It's true; even when you were at school she could tune into your thinking whenever she wanted and she often wanted. If you ever become a mother you'll be the same. I somehow was burdened with knowing mom was listening in. You spend the first twenty years of your life only thinking thoughts you think your mother would approve of, it does something to you. Sort of ruins you forever. Makes you want to devote your life to writing poems or something. Repairing toasters. Any anguished priesthood you could name. Then at a certain point you do a flip-flop, turn into a veritable lamb of warmth and softness. The universe begins to resemble a Superheroes comic book, and you are the reader. Taking away the sins of the world. For years you were plagued by impressions that there were certain important things you weren't supposed to know. Now you know those things are unknowable. You know everything you need to know the moment you need to know it. But you don't need to know that. As for me, I thought my parents were conspirators on a global scale, in league with all of nature and all of humanity in dragging me down screaming from heaven. Now I look at them and smile deeply. I'm my only conceivable enemy and we're going through a period of detente.

Cute little two-bar saxophone riff in the middle of a boring piano solo. Today I walked for miles on the hot pavement, barefoot, holding my sandals in my hand, my feet bleeding and dirty, and thought about my mind, as if it were my brain that had broken not my sandal strap. An unchained elephant is a dangerous thing. They'll uproot parking meters, trample flowerbeds, crash through the windows of health food stores. Chained, they become sad and deep and wise and gentle. A sort of Stalinism of the self. Now and then a mother discovers her own mind.

The eighth-century Buddhist poet Shantideva likened the mind to a wild elephant.

13. The Worst of People

Last night I had a drink with an old friend who told me that people
talk about me and I shuddered. She said at least four people have told her
that they love my writing but hate me. They talk about my string of
alleged betrayals and absence of sexual responsibility as if they knew me
intimately, and I sighed and said it's all true but exaggerated and that
I'm busy paying for all my sins, I burn night and day and I've tried
always, throughout it all, to do the right thing for myself and others.
I've been scrupulous, I said, even when I seem to have been anything
but scrupulous. She said she hoped the rumours were true because
she herself has lots of explosive affairs, but that's not the issue,
I said, people love to point at those who seem to be crueller and more
selfish than they, for then they don't have to point the finger at
themselves. My battle is with myself, I said, not with others, and
my own finger never points at anyone but myself. Things happen
to me, I always try my best, I constantly read books about how to be
a better person, great novels that reveal the secrets of the human
heart, and I practise selfless love, or try to, though the self is all.

I went home sad and lonely and sleep took its time in coming.
Over and over I relived that horrible weekend in the mountains,
my demons deliberately keeping oblivion at bay, for they wanted
me to know I was the worst of people, I had absolutely nothing to
offer the world, in fact the world would be an infinitesimally better
place if I simply shot myself. In the morning, surprisingly, all
seemed well again, and I had some almonds and coffee for breakfast.
I got tough with my mind and spent the day working hard, simply
sailed through the day with no hate in my heart for myself or anyone.

14. The CN Tower

People who hate us crowd into our dreams, people who want us
to know how much they hate us, who think they know us, who think
the way we were then and there is the way we will continue to be. They
don't think they could ever be wrong but they are always wrong.

We met for a drink last night, someone who used to share with me
a highly refined degree of amorous and scatological enthusiasms.
She said she had pinned on her wall a certain letter I sent her last year
so that she would be reminded daily what a rat I was, so that when
I finally called, and she knew I'd finally call, she would be instantly
on her guard. She smiled and blushed and said the day before I finally
called she'd removed the letter from the wall and thrown it out. A
coincidence, she said, and blushed again. But I was uncomfortable,
awkward, depressed. She looked so lovely I told her she was more lovely
in her wide-brimmed straw hat and fashionable red dress than a Mozart
string quartet and everyone in the bar was aware of her warmth and so on
but she complained quite rightly that I seemed bored, my eyes kept
shifting to the wall and the bar and the street though she'd just
returned from a lengthy tour of India and was full of interesting
adventures and observations to relate, and she knew I was interested
in India. Who isn't? We'd been friends and we enjoyed all the same things
but I'd failed to feel the same compulsion to draw nearer to her in the
spirit, we quarrelled, we developed radically conflicting views of the
same events, and she'd concluded that I was one who employed subtle
psychological methods for keeping people at arm's length. We left the
bar and walked along Yonge Street, midnight, hot, and I felt again
uncomfortable, there was nothing connecting us, everything had
gone, we found we couldn't even walk at the same pace, and suddenly
above our heads was the CN Tower, rising out of the mist, all colours.

15. My Grandmother Learns to Drive

There I was standing on the shore of a small lake in the Muskokas
and the sky, the clouds, the waves and the small boats, everything
was composed of tiny patches of coloured light and each patch
was a little being with its own little consciousness, and each
patch was swimming in a unified field of golden light. Even the
dreamer was composed of little patches of light swimming in
the same field of golden light, and my poor old grandmother
who was ninety and had never driven a car came by driving a car
and I climbed in and as she drove she drove slowly into a
snowdrift and stalled, she'd been doing pretty well until then.
So we got out of the car and sat in the snow and all around us
the snow was melting into miscellaneous little patches of white
and the earth was becoming warm and rich with new life.

With a finger I started digging little holes absently in the earth
and I touched something soft and round and buried, a young
mushroom, and it must have become aroused by my touch
for it slowly began to grow, pushing up through the soil,
and it grew and grew like a penis slowly becoming erect,
and when it had grown to its full height the earth around it
heaved as if with ecstasy and the mushroom shot a flurry of spores
out into the air and I looked at my grandmother and she smiled.

16. Blazing Nirvana

The mind of a child who knows he is dying opens with the radiance
of multiple moons and hovers without dream or thought over a heap
of Egyptian sarcophagi, a funnel-shaped column of erased existence.
For Life, dear Life, our own, our all, the fabulous flesh in which we
dwell, dully but apprehensive of an end of dullness, of a continuing
joyful amplification of consciousness, we know you'll never leave us,
for we are you and you are we, there can be nothing simpler, but it is
so easy to forget the hard edges of our lives are soft, the highest
mountains are nothing but forms of thought, multiple moons merely
hallucinations, the grade A variety that take eons to dissolve entirely.

And you and I go to see *Return of the Jedi* and I tell you that Zasep
the lonely lama went to see it and was suddenly overjoyed to hear the
"teddy bears who go running around in the forest with bows and arrows"
speaking Tibetan, although he managed to refrain from yelling out,
"Hey, that's my language," as understandable as such a spontaneous
exclamation of joy would be. And you asked me why a Buddhist priest
would go to see such a movie. He's young, I say, he's got a sense of
humour and a curiosity about the world he knows to be nothing but
forms of thought, the hard crust at the outer edge of blazing nirvana.
And you merrily remind me that you're going to Japan in the fall,
you're going to be selfconscious because you're so fair and tall,
and as usual I'll be staying at home sadly staring at a blank wall
and being swept away by my lonely sense of the spirit that is in all.

17. The Inchworm

There was an inchworm on the curb, one end stuck to the curb and the
other end inching up into the air like a tiny rearing stallion. I stepped out
of the car and you said Look, there's an inchworm, and I said Oh yes,
look at it. When we're dead we won't be able to look at inchworms
but they'll be able to look at us, crawl all over us, inch by inch.
They are strange and I do not like them but I wouldn't want to kill one,
would much prefer to kill a mosquito any day. I had a friend once who
swallowed not an inchworm or a mosquito but a dragonfly. He was riding
his bicycle with his mouth open and a dragonfly flew down his throat. If
you've ever seen a dragonfly larva go through the intricate process of
splitting its skin to make way for the emergence of its adult form then
watched its adult form hanging from the leaf like a smudge of snot
then go darting away across the summer sky you'd agree that it was
a senseless way for anything so beautiful to meet its death. Some say
for every insect we kill deliberately that's another incarnation we have
to suffer, we have to be born and get murdered once for every bug we
step on. But inchworms aren't insects, they are worms, little living
units of measure, that's why I don't want to kill them, each inchworm
is a little word of God's language. I am glad there are no footworms.

Or yardworms. In the morning I woke and remembered seeing the
inchworm on the curb and thought it an image from a dream. I thought I'd
dreamt that we had seen an inchworm. As I was pouring coffee you phoned
and said, Wasn't that a nice inchworm we saw yesterday? You mean
it wasn't a dream? I said. It was real, you said. Oh, I guess I woke up
thinking it was a dream, I said. It was like a dream, you said, it was
so clear the way the light was glistening on the curb and the worm and
there was something in the moment that made it all very dreamlike.

18. Blue Irises

It makes me feel lonely when I realize the past simply does not exist,
we simply talk as if it does. And of course there is no future. Nothing
but now, nothing ahead, nothing behind. There was a time when I felt
that writing was my life, now I don't know what I think until I think it.
My friend Walter says there is no subconscious so that if you do something
and only later find out why, you are fooling yourself. If a man chooses
blue irises to send to someone he loves and later remembers she associates
blue irises with someone else, he'd be a fool to berate himself, or bother
to look more deeply into the case, for it's simply that he forgot. Who
was it who said that he who knows there is no past and no future has
control over both? Perhaps it was my friend Walter. It's hard for me to
believe the things my inadequate mind tells me I used to believe. It's hard
for me to imagine anyone being the kind of person I remember having
been and later becoming the kind of person I now imagine myself to be.
No one can talk as if there is no future, is no past, the future and the past
have to be invented before we can begin to speak. Don't be misled. As if.
There's no reason for you to know that I am sitting here writing this
and resisting editing the movie concurrently running in my mind
simultaneously, resisting slowing it down and running it frame by frame.
It's true the sadness in my mind interests me, but don't expect me to try
to figure out why I'm sad. Nothing can be anybody's life. Peace to all!

Walter says he wants to be remembered for his poetry, he likes to think
of academics in universities a hundred years from now looking at his
verse and discovering hidden meanings. He says there is no subconscious
and I say there is no past or future, I'm not sure about the present, I'm the
man who sent blue irises to you and recalled too late you hate blue irises.

19. Terrible Storm on Lake Erie

It was Father's Day at the Seaway Hotel and everyone had the chicken
cordon bleu special. Mom didn't have anything to drink, but dad and his
two grown sons drank two beers each. Dad asked me if I had a five on me.
I did. He said give it to Jack, so I did, and dad handed me a neatly folded
ten. He said he found it on the street and when he found it he thought I'll
give it to my sons the struggling artists, so he did. Mom said Mr. Silver
had a heart attack and died, and I remembered scenes from his terrible
marriage. The time for instance he and his wife had a terrible fight
and he took his little motorboat straight out into Lake Erie in the middle
of a terrible storm. Everyone on the beach in silence watched him
disappear behind the black waves over and over again, his wife sobbing
and being held by the neighbours and the minister. But that was years ago
when Mr. Silver was young and had a romantic little moustache like Clark
Gable or Errol Flynn. He finally divorced his wife and married again and
now he's dead and his first wife is in a nursing home in Vancouver.

Mom and dad looked so wonderfully happy sitting there, white hair, happy
after forty years of marriage's ups and downs. I wondered why the
waitress didn't seem to be more thrilled to be waiting on them. She
didn't seem to notice their rare and simple beauty. There was a little
orchestra playing songs from old Fred Astaire movies and there were
other little families celebrating Father's Day but we were the best.

20. If I Were a Buddhist

I could accept my solitude all the time if I were a Buddhist, for it
is a lovely experience to accept the absolute and inevitable. But when
I manage to do so the experience is fleeting. Aloneness is absolute, but
I won't bore you or embarrass myself with listing the things I do to avoid
accepting anything as absolute. Buddhists say they pledge allegiance to their
breath rather than to the robber-like emotions and fickle thoughts that suck
you in and drown you. If I could do that I could perhaps learn to love and feel
compassion for everyone without discrimination, the poor and lonely
that populate this city. And I could love and feel compassion for myself
without necessarily wanting to take myself home and sleep with me.
Perhaps I could learn to trust myself, to see myself as an old friend
whose tear-choked voice is as familiar as dust on the doorknob.

Perhaps I would not be so aggressive with myself if I were a Buddhist
but it seems that to be kind to myself is simply not my nature. People
can't force themselves to change. Perhaps I could lovingly encourage
myself to be nicer to myself but then it's not really nicer to myself
I want to be, nor less aggressive. I should be grabbing myself by the
hair and saying look buddy, smarten up, quit allowing yourself to be
sucked in by all that emotion and thought. Just breathe. In and out.
Perhaps if I were a Buddhist instead of merely curious I'd give up this
endless canoeing down every river of my mind, those rivers have no
substance anyway, and the scenery's always the same. And perhaps I'd
stop trying to solve all my little problems. And all of this would happen
like leaves springing in the spring or falling in the fall, my feeling
of caring whether I'm right or wrong, of my stake in my own territory,
my own life, my own so-called self. And I would immediately renounce
all but the insanity of being alive in this infernal moment, swimming
in the soup du jour boiling away under the mind's manhole cover.

21. Lion in the Road

It was lying in the intersection of Bloor and Avenue Road, a giant
lion larger than six elephants, each tooth the size of a fire hydrant
but sharper. It was having a snooze, it took up the entire intersection
and its tail stretched out lazily all the way down to Bedford Road. Its eyes
were open but not seeing much, not noticing the incredible traffic jam,
incredible because no one was honking, incredibly quiet traffic jam: cars
were making cautious U-turns and heading quietly back the way they came.
Basically though it was business as usual. Fashionable ladies in chic
clothing stores weren't coming out to stare, they just kept trying on
the latest fashionable dresses. People in chic restaurants continued
eating lunch, nothing about giant lions in the newspaper, so why look?
A Toronto newspaper columnist and a famous novelist from Connecticut
came out of Bemelman's where they'd been drinking white housewine,
came out without paying and walked by the lion without even a glance.
It was as if the lion had been lying there since the days of the Family
Compact. Or at least since Hugh Garner got banned from the Press Club.
There was the sense that the lion hadn't been officially approved for
notice. Toronto's like that, the sort of city where the day after the famous
travel writer came out with a story complaining that people in Toronto
never talk to strangers everyone started talking to strangers. Someone
I didn't know actually spoke to me in an elevator. And I answered! But
back to the lion. Even tourists and conventioneers with Hi-My-Name-Is
stickers on their lapels merely glanced at the lion before turning away
to point out to each other noteworthy examples of Victorian architecture.
Nobody seemed nervous, surprised, concerned, nobody seemed to be rushing
off to phone the cops or the zoo, though it's obvious this lion didn't escape
from any zoo, no zoo in the world could handle lions this size. Fortunately,
it didn't seem to be hungry, though I wondered what it had been eating,
a lion that size could eat sixteen dogs a day easy and I didn't see any dogs.

So I sat on a bench in front of the Royal Ontario Museum and wondered
what it was about me, why do things that most people scarcely notice
affect me so, why can't I be like everyone else and simply turn and go
back the way I came without honking? Why do I always have to give a
damn? And as I watched, the lion stiffened, began ascending into the sky,
became smaller and smaller and floated away behind a mass of cloud
in the shape of a lion. In no time traffic was back to normal. Honk!

22. The Moons of Jupiter

I used to think so-and-so and so-and-so were the closest couple but now
I think it's Paul and Diana. Have they become closer or have I
begun to see them differently? We all know that couples are unbearable,
they cling to each other like Titanic survivors. Yet it's enchanting to sense
the fire between Paul and Diana when they suddenly sense it themselves,
the big slow spark when their eyes connect from across the room. Tonight
we drank a bottle of scotch, the three of us, sat on the back porch watching
the sky change over Toronto, you can see Lake Ontario from their place,
and a full moon was suddenly climbing the CN Tower and Diana said oh,
look at the moon, and the stars were beginning to appear, and Paul
got out a tiny pair of binoculars and said last night you could see the
moons of Jupiter but not tonight. And I looked at Paul to see if he was
fooling me but he looked serious. So did Diana. Can you see Jupiter's moons
with only a small pair of binoculars? Was I the butt of a joke? Can you
see the delicate magnetism between two people if you're the third?

Or does it take a special kind of magnetism? I kept dropping hints, so much
was I enjoying myself, that I might be coaxed to sit up all night with them
and watch the sun come up over the lake and they said they've never seen
the sun come up over the lake and had no intention of starting now. I was
disappointed, maybe they weren't enjoying themselves as much as I was.
The conversation was brilliant, at least I thought it was. We talked about
everything, with all the ease and brilliance that was in the air, and Diana
brought out vanilla ice cream and fresh strawberries. Oh, it was lovely!
Was it because I was alone? If you had been with me would they have
liked me better, thought it a great idea to stay up all night and watch the
sun come up in the morning? No, but I soon sensed they wanted me to
leave so they could do whatever it is that lovers do when they're alone.
I noticed that when I returned from the washroom they were embracing
and when they heard me returning they reluctantly moved apart so I left
and I know right now I don't know why I'm telling you all this, I only
know that my mind simply insists that I grab my pen and start writing.
Maybe it's just that I need to say something and this is all I have to say.

23. Separation Anxiety

There are two major anxieties known to love's holy pilgrims, but seldom
do they coinhabit the lover's psyche simultaneously. Performance
anxiety is something one knows about and thinks about but seldom
talks about. Separation anxiety, however, is the theme of the noblest
verse. She is a wonderful person, the woman with whom I am spending
the evening, and although I am enjoying our conversation, in fact her
very presence, the hound of my mind keeps sniffing along the path that
leads to splendid memories of you. I yank it back with a tug of its leash
and it stays a minute then off it goes again, tail wagging, nose down, and
this time I let it go. It's my body, I discover, that sad animal I lug around
every day, and it is sad because it cannot understand where you've gone,
and I will not mention you to my friend for I know if I do she will start
asking for intimate details, and she will criticize me for longing for you.

She will tell me romantic love is the opiate of the masses, she will invite
me to grow up and become enlightened, she will not understand in the
slightest the intense pleasure only we can share. And as we sit here
talking I feel my breath rising and falling, and my desire for you, deeper
than thought, spreads from my heart to all parts of my body like pumping
blood. This is separation anxiety, and I write this with little irony, little
anxiety in fact, little embarrassment, only because in my mind you are
feeling the same. There is nothing I feel that you don't feel as well: an
hypothesis I'll retain until it proves unworkable, degrading or dangerous.
At least this is what I say tonight, although I must admit that last night
I wrote in my notebook that I'd like to tear my brain into little pieces
then glue the pieces back together again in an entirely different way.

24. Dogs That Never Disappear

Mom and dad went out one day and I took my new puppy into the
yard and we chased each other around for awhile. I could hear the
phone ringing and I decided not to answer it but it kept on ringing
and I thought it might be important so I thought it would be okay
to leave the pup alone for a moment and ran to answer the phone.
It was a wrong number and when I went back out the pup was gone.
He'd just wandered off. For the rest of the afternoon I walked around
the neighbourhood calling the puppy's name even though he didn't have
a name yet. I just made it up. And I never found him, never saw that
pup again. I'm writing this for you, for you and your crazy pain.

Now I'm all grown up and although I still like dogs I would never
want to own one. I feel sorry for people when I see them out walking
their dogs, they always look as if they wish they were elsewhere,
inside watching television for instance, as if they really somehow
don't like their dogs. But, strangely, their dogs never disappear.
You probably thought this poem was going to be morbid but it was
only sentimental and transparently metaphorical. Turned out to be
a dog of a poem. An elaborate justification for not having a dog.
Why should I have a dog? I already have a dog and its name is me.

25. Airpipe to the Surface

What I miss is your unsurpassed friendship. How long has it been, two months? I feel so bereft it's natural I should forget you or try to but you won't let me, you revivify me as you say with your disembodied calls. I want to let my blood spurt from severed arteries and watch it running in rivulets to the sewer, my mind gently detached. In the morbid stories of Cornell Woolrich there are elements of intense romantic agony and I become all woozy with sympathy for the young woman who agrees to be buried alive in a coffin in place of her boyfriend, a coffin with an airpipe leading to the surface, and the valve is gradually closed. When she's finally rescued her boyfriend holds her and tells her he never knew there could be love like that in all the world. She says there is, there is.

And yet it seems I should be writing as if I were going to die tomorrow, though my writing seems to be losing its ambition. No longer do I seem to have a need to impress myself, unless it's by no longer having a need to impress myself. Everything's fine here. The radioactive world either will or won't survive the current nuclear crisis. One finds oneself no longer trying to impress the world, no longer taking the world or oneself seriously. One finds oneself seeing through the tiny holes into the radiance out of which we come and into which we go.

26. Transparencies

I was watching a movie on television, occasionally checking my
watch. I wanted to be at the terminal to meet you as you got off
the late bus from Montreal. I was thinking of all the men who ever
ruined the lives of the women they loved and I kept practising
opening my heart and letting you fly away, you have the brains
to find your way back if you want. Usually I don't like writing
that doesn't deal with the intensely personal, writers who don't
reveal themselves with every breath usually don't interest me,
the only information I need is information about the naked
human heart, anything else I can dial the Metro Library or
access Infoglobe. My idea of torture is so naïve, like a propaganda
movie made in wartime, where no one gets killed, they fight
with fists and angry hearts. I think of being tied in a room
for hours with nothing to drink and a man coming in and pouring
a pitcher of ice water on the floor, and all I can do is sit there
watching it evaporate. As for the real thing, fingernail rip-outs,
nipple severance, I wonder if I'd have the courage to withstand it.
You say you have to know you're going to die and the only thing
you have left is the power to keep your mouth shut and nothing
they can do will take that power away from you. I don't want to be a
superman, but it would be nice to have the kind of mind that could soar
above the most horrendous torture, though I hope it never has to.

You phoned before I left and said the bus was early. I said hop in a
cab and see you soon. You did, and you arrived, and you stayed, and we
loved each other again with rare felicity, two babies in one womb.

27. Windsurfers

Since everything is plausible this summer, I've no idea what
I'm doing, where I'm going, my mind is dimly lit and empty.
You've heard this before. We stayed up for hours looking at each other
and smiling, then fell asleep. In the morning our eyes opened at
the same moment like four cherry blossoms on one bough. Irony
is no longer a large part of my life, imagine that! Everything is
changing, everything is plausible, and I now see that wisdom
and knowledge can never co-exist. Oh madame, I embrace you
with all the spring breezes and starry nights of all my lives,
with all the darkness of this radiant moment, with what I hope
is the blindness of wisdom, more than instinct, less than intuition.

And since everything is plausible this summer, I suggest a quiet
part of the beach, the stony part, less crowded than the sandy,
and there is no one there. There are two kinds of people: those
who like the stony part and those who like the sandy. And there's
my friend Andy, he likes the Sandy. Andy Panda and Sandy Stone.
Please don't show this poem to anyone. Windsurfers, four of them,
come racing out from behind the distant rocky point, and one turns
abruptly and heads for shore, the others stopping to watch him go
then turning and heading farther out. I guess he just remembered
he had to make an urgent call. And so we eat cherries and spit the
pits among the stones. The water is cold, the sun hot, the breeze
cool, the sky blue, your breasts radiant with love's intelligence,
I enjoy my confusion as it is, and refuse to view it with irony.

28. Late Afternoon Rainfall

It started raining. Fire trucks, ambulances and police cars screamed
down the street. I ducked under a tree and saw on the fence a poster
advertising a concert being given by my brother eight days before.
Caught in yet another torrent. Sometimes my problems become even
too trivial for me. When I was in the country I longed to be in the city
and now I'm in the city I want to be back in the country. We took,
yesterday, potato chips, cherries, mineral water, peanuts and plums
to the beach. We let the sun burn into our bones. You came out of the
primal foam, stood by a large rock and smiled, your wet hair shining,
long neck wet, water running down your shoulders. I said you'd never
see yourself as clearly as I saw you right then and your eyes flashed.
I saw you standing there in the sunny void, on the stony sandy beach,
with the Picasso blue waves coming in out of nowhere and the sailboats
out on the horizon and no one around, I saw you the way you will be
always in eternity, I opened the cage of my heart and you flew away.

Ah, no use writing about yesterday. This morning you called a cab and
off you went to the airport to fly to Lisbon or somewhere. I found myself
a bit disoriented, spent the whole day trying to figure out how to
spend the day, couldn't work, went to a movie and walked out after
half an hour. You said you didn't want to be a bad influence on me,
I said that would be impossible, but for the first twelve hours after
you leave I feel incapacitated by an icy unfamiliar emptiness.

29. Midsummer Garden Party

For most of my life I've lived in Southern Ontario but have never travelled
this route before, the longer route by rail from Toronto, the train heading
through Guelph, Georgetown, Kitchener, as if I were looking at my right
ear from behind my back, practising being in the moment, not desiring
anything but what is in the moment one is in. There is a demon that causes
spectacular coincidences to arise and causes one to think of enchantment.
I was walking through the stacks in the Metro Library and a book fell
at my feet. It was Arthur Koestler's *Roots of Coincidence*. Of course
I read the book, and later read another Koestler book which was a
biography of an Austrian biologist named Paul Kammerer who committed
suicide at forty-five after being accused of faking an experiment. He was
the first scientist of our era to take coincidence seriously and kept a log
of coincidences for twenty years, and when I phoned the bookstore to
order Koestler's biography of him the sales clerk said: What a coincidence!
The book is right here in my hand! I've been reading it all day! Kammerer
believed in the genetic inheritance of acquired characteristics and you
said it would be interesting to know if his children became interested
in coincidence, or if they killed themselves at forty-five, or if they faked
scientific experiments. And as the train reaches an automated carwash
in Kitchener the conductor says this way out please but I decide I don't
need a carwash and so stay on, attending to the pureness of the moment
as it expands around the person attending to his presence in it, as if the
moment has its own mind which is subject to flattery and pure affection.
I've never seen Southern Ontario from this angle. Other moments from
random days and nights of your life and other lives bleed into the
moment you're in and time flows in unpredictable patterns, service is
terrible, sandwiches stale, but my heart is at peace and my mind too.

Later, at a garden party at Geoffrey and Goldie Rans' place which backs
onto Gibbon Park, I met people I haven't seen in years, and nice friendly
folks I've never met before. And together, as dark approached, we sat
quietly and watched an hour of fireworks exploding in the summer sky.

30. God's Way of Remaining Anonymous

I overimbibed at the opening of Gord's show at the Embassy Gallery
in the east end of London, Ont., listening to people from the west end
complaining about the east end, how depressing, the wrong end of town.
It would have been better if you'd been there, but I want you to know I
thought about you, and remembered asking you what you thought of the
theory that coincidence surrounds us all the time but we just don't
notice it, and when we start to notice it then we notice it all the time.
You didn't like that theory, you preferred to believe coincidence
only occurs in the lives of those with powerful spiritual energy,
a vacuum around which streams of coincidence create a vortex.
Lawrence speaks about it, you said, and I said I didn't understand.
So everyone (except you) went back to Greg Curnoe's place and I
dozed off while watching a horror movie with Greg, Sheila, Owen,
Galen, Zoë, and Murray Favro drove me to the train station where I
bumped into Sandy Sparks who was also at the party the night before,
and Sandy and I took the train back to Toronto, past the late-afternoon
tulip trees, turkey tents and tiny towns. I remembered you saying the hidden
music of coincidence turns everyday life from prose to verse. You were
watching a religious program on television one night and a woman got up
and said, Coincidence is God's way of remaining anonymous. Sandy Sparks
told me about the death of her mother, and her visits to her father in the
nursing home in Guelph, the special responsibilities of being an only child,
and the conductor told us the alimony he has to pay is finally worth the
freedom he enjoys, and an older woman whose husband, as soon as he'd
recovered from his heart bypass operation, divorced her, said she was
on her way to Sudbury to attend the funeral of her brother who died of a
brain tumour, and she was curious about Sandy Sparks and me, had we
just met or were we lovers and if so how long? We both blushed. The woman
had an hour's stopover in Toronto and wanted to spend some time with us
in the bar but we wished her luck at the funeral and said we had to go.

Sandy Sparks invited me to her place for a Coke and said if I paid the cab
she'd give me a spare fan she had, for I'd been complaining about the heat.
When I got home I plugged it in, it worked beautifully, and you phoned
from Kansas City, and reminded me you'd be flying to Toronto on Tuesday.

31. The Snake

Here, dear friend, is that tough and juicy little string of poems in prose
I promised you, and you will notice immediately that it has neither
head nor tail while at the same time it could be said without injustice
that it is all head and all tail! Such convenience! We can cut wherever
we want: me my dreaming, you the manuscript, the reader his reading!
Remove one vertebra and the two halves of this tortured fantasy will
close the gap without a gasp. Hack it to pieces and you will find that each
piece could exist on its own. And in the hope that some of the pieces will
please and amuse you I dedicate to you the entire snake. Confession time:
in flipping once again through the pages of that famous book we both
admire, you know the one I mean, famous that is as far as you and I and
certain of our friends are concerned, the idea came to me to try to apply
to modern urban life the method the author found so strangely effective
in portraying life in antiquity in such a strangely picturesque way. For,
in moments when ambition kicks sand in our faces, who has not dreamt
of a method of writing strong and supple enough to handle the lyrical
movements of the soul, the ripples of our dreams, and the gutwrenching
contractions of our conscience? This ideal has become an obsession,
a hungry bird hatched from the egg of my persistent brooding over the
lives of the people of this crazy city and the crisscrossing of their
countless connections. Have you never felt tempted to transpose into song
the insane chatter of the characters in your books, and to express in
lyrical prose the heartbreaking suggestions such chatter brings to us
through the smoke and the unspeakable mist of the nonstop street?

If you know what I mean. But my jealousy has failed to bring me to bliss.
As soon as I started work I found I was straying far from the model I'd
set for myself, that mysterious and brilliant book we love so well.
I saw that I was making something singularly different, an accident
which serves nevertheless only to humiliate a spirit such as mine,
a spirit which regards the greatest accomplishment a poet could possibly
accomplish would be to accomplish just what he set out to accomplish.

After Baudelaire's dedication of his *Petits Poèmes en Prose*.

32. Gossip

The squirrels and the blackbirds seemed to enjoy each other's presence
as I took off my shirt in the sunny park and watched myself slowly turning
pink, went through a couple of French lessons in that book you gave me,
then got up and walked to the office where I worked till the sun went down.
I took my story to my editor's place and we chatted in her garden for an
hour. I remembered being on the bus one day last week, heading out to
Victoria Park Collegiate to teach a class of teenage poets. Kris Nakamura,
one of my students, got on at the third stop wearing her brown beret, and
didn't notice me till she got past my seat. I turned and said hi and she
came up and sat beside me. I chatted away about Roy Kiyooka's new poetry
and even quoted sections from memory, then Kris rang the bell and said,
"Sorry, Dave, I can't come to class today, I have a doctor's appointment,"
and when she got off I noticed she'd left behind her brown beret so I
opened the window and when the light turned and the bus took off I waited
until we were abreast of her and called out the window, "Here's your
brown beret, Kris," and tossed it. She smiled as she watched it fly in its
brownish arc and land at her feet like a pear from a tree. And then later
as I was going into the teacher's room for coffee a kid standing at his
locker smiled a pimply smile and called out, "That was a good toss, sir."

So I asked my editor if she'd seen me walking past her house last week.
Remember? We were walking back from the beach, and as we walked by
she looked out the window, then abruptly turned away. She said it was
very strange, she was thinking about me and looked out the window
and there I was, "hustling some broad." She said she wished she'd had
her glasses so she could have seen the broad. She said she always had the
knack of looking out at just the right moment. I said I didn't really think
she'd seen. "Good," she said, "you weren't intended to think I saw you."
Of course I objected, I said I wasn't hustling some broad, I was merely
walking along the street with a dear old friend who happened to be a
beautiful woman. She said she told everyone at the office she'd seen me
walking down the street hustling some broad. What a gossip! Thank God
she didn't have her glasses. If she'd seen you more clearly she'd have had
a better story to spread. And I think I'll go back to the park this afternoon
and watch the squirrels and blackbirds enjoying each other's presence.

33. Nightmares

Naked woman kicked to death. Front page of the *Toronto Sun*. Picture
of woman in happier times. Picture of suspect being carted away. I've
just eaten a big meal; I fainted twice today so it must be time to get
back to eating. I stood there at the *Sun* box for a moment, thinking
back to my days as a police reporter, how I would have loved to have
belted that story and those photos into the city editor five scary
minutes before deadline, how I would have pestered the cops until
they finally confessed, yes, it looks as if he kicked her to death.
And I would have said how many times do you figure he kicked her?
And if they had said they had no idea, I would have said fifty? And they'd
have said oh at least. A hundred? And they'd have said maybe. What great
fun it was to approach the grief-stricken father and ask for a picture
of his little girl who had just been flattened by a beer truck and if he
hesitated you told him you didn't want to have to run a morgue shot.

Ten years later my nightmares are carefully constructed, like formula
stories by pulp writers in the thirties and forties. And, ahem, I'm
beginning to realize I have certain (non-violent) psychotic tendencies
and of course prefer writers who talk on and on about themselves, even
if they don't realize they're doing so. I like to shave off my beard or grow
a new one on a whim, I like to change faces from time to time, to be
ruthless one day and full of fear and remorse the next. I'm glad others
are obsessed with the injustices we see all around us, it leaves me free
in my own way to bite at the barbed wire of miracles that pens us in hell,
the cruel fork of coincidence that drags us into the kangaroo court of
daily insanity and bliss in that majestic courthouse at the bottom of the
deepest sea, and each night I love to surface and read you my daily poem.
I don't want to deify you but you know I want you to be there where your
care can fill me with the courage to plunge more deeply into that sea.

34. The Road to Thunder Bay

I was waiting at the Islington station for a bus to take me to the airport and
a red-haired man in a uniform was waiting for the same bus. Customs official.
He had a bag of cherries and tossed one at a little sparrow who didn't notice
where it landed. He was fat, had bushy sideburns, he offered me the bag, I
took a couple of cherries and ate them. The bus came. For hours I'd felt you
flying across the sky. I read about a baseball player in Japan who was in a
hitting slump. When the reporters asked him what the matter was he said
he couldn't figure it out, he could see the ball okay, was in good health,
and was having regular bowel movements. And there you were collecting
your luggage and we stood close to each other and smiled shyly and you
asked if you might give me a small kiss on the cheek and I said oh okay
and we went back to my place and drank red wine and I read you a few
poems from the past few days, when we are in love we always have an
audience for our poetry said Jack Spicer, and it wasn't long before our
little thoughts were undressing and embracing like little people, and I
recalled your favourite pie was lemon meringue while mine was rhubarb.

Next day Ross picked us up in his Ferrari and off we went up the long road
to Thunder Bay, you in the jump seat pulling sweaters out of Ross's bag
and putting them on and me trying to tie something around your head
so your hair wouldn't blow so much. "You are really precious to me,"
I wrote, inspired, on a slip of paper and handed it back to you, and you
threw your arms around me with glee. I'm not sure Ross liked that. He
always wanted to be the supremely dominant male. We drank Mumm's
as we drove and I kept turning around to see your pretty smile, though
I said I was turning around to make sure you hadn't fallen out. Later
you said Ross had been flashing eyes at you through the mirror all the
way. As only he can. I had funny premonitions about the trip, three on an
island, knife in the water, a beautiful woman and two competitive men,
both of whom would do anything to be the centre of attention. Right away
I decided to give up. We stopped in Thunder Bay and loaded up with groceries
and seven more bottles of Mumm's and Ross went to visit an old fisherman
dying in the local hospital of fishbone in the throat. We picked up the boat
at the marina, sped to the island, and I became an anonymous Zen monk,
and stayed that way for the duration of our stay and perhaps still am.

35. Beauty and Remoteness

Other islands visible from the shore of an island in Lake Superior, visible
from the cottage where you could sit on the roof all night and watch
the stars and in the morning see the sunrise ripening like a Niagara peach
across the sky and freshwater sea, the cedars, pine and fabulous granite
bedrock, the prehistoric lava flows. Ross says it is his favourite place,
he's been coming here since childhood, and that rubs off, we begin to
feel it too, the centre of the world, and we walk barefoot on the bedrock
and you speak of how you've always loved the Canadian Shield, even more
than your native Florida coral, but somehow beauty and remoteness
tend to depress me, I begin having black fantasies about lost childhood
loves, people entombed alive and found dead with fingernails bleeding,
subtle ironies begin to escape me, I begin to lose the courage to be
completely wrong, I find myself worrying about my wit and wisdom,
I begin to think of myself as a fool which robs me of the right to be
a fool without giving it a troublesome thought, and my thought becomes
superficial, the little bare toes of my thinking not wanting to touch the
fabulous bedrock, afraid of being grounded, afraid of snakes, and one
thought begins clinging to the other, afraid of drowning or falling through
the cracks into even greater hell, thoughts begin swallowing each other
instead of their own tails, I watch the crows, the snowy white gulls,
I walk around the island looking for rattlers, hoping to find one.

There will always be wars because the individual human being refuses
to do battle with himself says my friend the Druid, and I begin to feel
I have been crucified and taken down from the cross, placed in the tomb,
and am waiting for the angels to roll away the stone. The Warrior of
Mixed Metaphor, my face still and alive in the dark, smiling of course,
for the angels will never forsake me. Why do we gladly want to be born
again for the sake of the other? Why do we think we can be rescued by
those who are drowning? And why is the spirit so demanding? Why do we
gladly tear our lives to shreds in the gamble that love will be pure and
constantly evolving into finer planes of being? A tender electrocution,
all the things a lover wants to hear, for the sake of the miracle we see
on the horizon like the fuzzy red rim of the morning sun that will never
rise no matter how we pray. I allow myself to feel sick and full of fear,
but not to the point where anyone would notice it. My mind is a robin
pulling fear from the stubborn ground. I know all this is mine, but I want
to examine first the remote but dazzling possibility that it may be yours.

36. In the Buffalo Airport

In the Buffalo Airport I began talking to a man who seemed utterly strange, friendly but refusing to tell me anything about himself, what he did for a living, where he was from, where he was going, why. My curiosity was growing wild. I asked him about love, and his answers were truly peculiar. Did he love his father, mother, sister, brother? "I have no father, mother, sister, brother," he said, clear-eyed, smiling, but without irony. Friends? "Friends?" he said. "Friends? That is a word that is totally unknown to me." When I asked if he had feelings for his native country he said he didn't even know where to locate it on the map. And when I mentioned love of the beautiful, he said he would be delighted to love beauty but beauty is an eternal principle and therefore impossible to love or hate. Money he said he despised. But when I asked him then what it was he did love, if anything, he pointed out the window and said, "I love clouds, the marvellous clouds."

There was a little child, just a toddler, wandering around, his parents watching closely from a distance, and everyone making a big fuss of him. And a little old woman, wrinkled and all shrivelled up, approached the child, smiled at him, held out her weak and shapeless arms to him. But the child became terrified, began struggling to free himself from the woman's arms, began screaming and hollering at the top of his lungs until his embarrassed parents picked him up and took him away. And the woman went back to her seat, back to her unyielding solitude, and began quietly sobbing, and I took a seat close enough to hear her talking to herself. "Ah," she said, between moans, "for miserable old women like me the time has long passed when we could please even the most innocent, and we horrify those we wish to love."

After "L'Étranger" and "Le Désespoir de la Vieille" from Baudelaire's *Petits Poèmes en Prose*.

37. The Sea Captain

My life has become Zen simple. I don't want to clutter it up with owning
boats, cottages, islands. Look at Ross: everything anyone else has he has
to have and more and so he has a wife, a house, two kids, three cars,
four trailers, five canoes, two windsurfers, a sailboat, a powerboat,
an island in Lake Superior and little pieces of women all over the world.
Don't get me wrong, I love the guy, we're skipping along the waves,
he's complaining about people who come to his island and expect to be
waited on, and we hit a big wave and you get drenched. He becomes a
slave, he says, and you come up to the front and sit between us. We see
docked in Thunder Bay the old blue ship that had passed as we sunbathed
on the westernmost rock of the island that morning, you in your string
bikini, me naked, Ross tending to the bacon and eggs. The ship had come
from the back side of a distant island, around the east side, apparently
tried to get into Thunder Bay by the wrong channel, turned around,
passed us and tried another channel. It sat so low in the water we figured
it must be hauling oil down below. And there safe in the harbour it was
sitting high and empty. Ready for more. It was from Sarnia and you slyly
smiled, remembering our strange rendezvous in Sarnia a week earlier.

Toronto. There was a moment of strangeness when the door slammed
and the bus took off, you with it, and I walked slowly home alone in the
slanting rays of the morning sun, past the anti-nuke protestors still
sleeping peacefully in their bags at Queen's Park. Later I took a nap
and dreamt I was a Sea Captain and ordered several dozen huge lemon
meringue pies to be served to my crew as a special bonus. Meringue
was everywhere, we were covered in it. And it was you, I realized sadly,
upon awakening. Even now I touch you in your absence and feel the
tear-filled eye in the centre of your body tremble, sigh and jabber
in tongues. My sleeping mind appears to think of you as lemon pie
but this is not as bad as it may seem. My dreams know little of psyche
and symbol, alchemy and the mysterium coniunctionis. But still I feel that magic
eye, the gentle human pressure as it opens and closes, the fainting swirl
of perfection and the bluntly bitter taste of your inevitable absence.

38. Over the Rainbow

This is my day to be all wrapped up in my daughters, we sit talking, they
are magnetic as the moons of Mars, alert with naked eyes, I reach out and
touch the hair of the older, make it bounce a little, and say I bet the boys
enjoy touching your hair like that, and she says, sadly, Craig did, and the
younger sighs and rolls her eyes. Mom says you're driving the boys wild,
I say to the younger, do you have any special techniques? And she denies it,
not wild, she says. The younger (but taller) is said to take after me, the
older after mom. I open a new roll and start snapping pictures, in the garden
among the roses, in the subdued light among the houseplants, the two
together, each alone, and we talk more clearly than we have for years,
we find we are in agreement about the varied states of our lives. I lightly
pat the older on the bum; she says, daddy, please don't do that, I'm almost
all grown up. She smiles with contentment. She's eighteen. Days like today
sneak up on me, I begin to feel uncomfortable, gummy and anxious in the
heart, I become like those European exiles you see spending the remainder
of their lives in the bars of remote tropical islands, and their misery
is even more miserable because of all the heavenly beauty that surrounds it.

I remind them that tomorrow is their parents' twentieth anniversary
and they say it seems much longer than that, it seems as if you've been
away almost twenty years. The house, the new one in which I never lived,
seems familiar, it is as if I have planted the flowers and vegetables, the cat
whose crushed leg has been pinned by the vet and who is pregnant and
whose last litter I watched being born at dawn, everyone else asleep, seems
to know me. The house is magnetic and peaceful, unlike anything else in my
life, but I know I can't make myself really belong here, and I must go, and I
leave books, *Sons and Lovers*, *Women in Love*, *The Rainbow*, and I explain
my choices, and suggest they read the books in the order they were written,
slowly, chapter by chapter, as if each chapter were a short story, and as I
leave both reach for *Sons and Lovers* (sounds as if it's about boys). And I
return to where I came from, where my most basic predicaments are laid
bare at my naked faithful uncomplaining feet, I return to a place that is not
magnetic or peaceful but for me a more magic place where angels roll away
the stone and eternity breathes, far from those I love. Here where my step
is slow and careful and I surrender myself to death's little list of desires
like a sweating beer-bellied accordionist in an all-night polka band.

39. How to Be Your Own Butcher

The theme of all great art: it's nice to be alive, and no matter how great
your suffering the earth will wait forever to take your flesh and bones.
So it's nice to be alive and well-fed too and to be able to spend the entire
day in the public library. I'm one of the lucky ones. How can I be neurotic?
Of course it's the lucky ones who are neurotic, not the ones who are working
on blast furnaces, in dark wobbly coal mines, or worse watching their kids
starve. But just to spend the day sitting around the library, watching people,
reading aimlessly but fruitfully, drifting, looking at the photographic
exhibits, the display from the Spanish embassy. A waterbed salesman in a
business suit is reading *A Practical Guide for the Beginning Farmer* and
there is a sign reading HOW TO BE, the sign's on a shelf containing all the
titles that start with the words how to be: *How to Be an Inventor, How to Be
a Complete Clown, How to Be a Disc Jockey, How to Be a Father, How to Be a
Fix-it Genius Using Seven Simple Tools, How to Be a Friend People Want to
Be Friends With, How to Be a Movie Star....* The waterbed salesman stood up
and walked over as I picked up a book entitled *How to Be Your Own Butcher*
and I laughed and turned to him blindly and said, "Looks like this book
is for the ultimate masochist!" And he looked horrified and turned and
walked away and only then did I notice he had a steel hook for a right hand.

"Commercial, but listenable," commented Max Ferguson on the radio this
morning, after playing a record by Switzerland's most famous yodeller,
there were quite a few interesting stories in the paper this morning, and
when I think about it I think I know quite a lot about how to be, frankly.
To write openly and without artifice is a magnificent gesture born of lovely
desperation. As Anna Akhmatova put it as her friends were dying in the
streets or at the front, "One hope the poorer, I'll be one song the richer."
Have no theories to hide behind, I tell myself, no dramatic stage for your
petty little ego, avoid suffering only by becoming supremely conscious of
the nature of suffering and let yourself be overwhelmed by it, and above all
let yourself sail alone on the ocean of insanity known as the poetic life.
Before coming into the library I saw a man (he possessed all his limbs)
bicycling along with a cigar in his mouth, a large portable radio set on his
crossbar and blaring away, and a large coloured picture of Jesus pasted to the radio.

40. Christian Wildflowers

Nothing can bother me this summer for there's nothing I can do about
anything, except to try to get a nice tan and let my beard grow. The agents
of Lucifer in Moscow and Washington can destroy my dreams and those
of my children and everyone at any moment but that just increases my
desire to be quiet and peaceful and allow my heart to blossom all it can.
I sit in the sun, eat ice cream, write and wonder. CHRIST IS COMING, says
the scrawled sign pasted on the back of the man walking by. He's about thirty,
blue hair, pink beard, blonde eyes, looks quite bright, as if he might
be a TA in the English department, but he's wearing flowing red robes
and although I've just been reading something about the end of the world
and although I know you're not supposed to smile at or talk to religious
fanatics in public places I can't resist smiling at him and saying, "Can't
come soon enough to suit me!" He looks shocked! He looks at me as if he
thinks I'm nuts! But maybe he's learned that look from the way people look
at him. Or maybe he's forgotten he has that sign on his back, or what it says.
He doesn't seem crazy to me and I hope I don't to him. Even in this peaceful
smug provincial land there is latent rage and you know how horrible it'd be,
as bad as Russia, Spain, or Germany at their respective nightmarish worst, if
suddenly we could shoot anyone we wanted without fear of punishment, right?
Anyone could kill or be killed at any time, smoking guns on the street and
leering faces. Only the truly compassionate would be able to resist the
temptation. I'd resist and the CHRIST IS COMING fellow would resist. You
would resist. In fact you say your father always said he'd rather live under
the worst totalitarian government than in a state of anarchy, which I fully
understand. I'd be shot for sure, just like Lorca, if I'm not flattering
myself, for people always complain they never know when I'm being sarcastic,
ironic, or merely making little jokes. I make people feel uncomfortable,
they say my sense of humour is far too subtle for my own good, they say I'll
never die in bed, unless I'm shot in bed. But no one would ever shoot you!

Yet today as well I'm thinking of wild flowers, I think there are wild flowers
in my heart, flowers small and gentle but truly wild like the beasts of the
tropical forest, and all over Southern Ontario wild flowers are blooming
wildly. Consider the wild flowers of the field, flowers being wild every day
and not just on weekends. It's nice to know that flowers can be wild. I think
I too am wild at heart, wild like a flower. Imagine, all over the countryside,
in sunlit meadows and in the darkest dampest woods, flowers growing wild,
those little bright flowers so wild night and day. Yesterday, alas, I read a
book of poems by my friend Walter and it was so good I decided to swear
off writing forever! I felt like Picasso's dad! I wanted to sell my typewriter,
to give someone a hundred bucks to push me in front of the Metro! But this
gave way to serenity! Today, a miracle! Wild flowers growing in my heart!

41. Geneva Violets

A man with a pair of binoculars around his neck was standing on the corner
in the shade of an elm, he was staring at you as we approached, he was
obviously deeply smitten, he continued staring at you as we passed, and so
I looked back at him and said, "Why don't you check her out with your
binoculars?" It was intended to be a benevolent remark, a joke in fact,
but he looked deeply insulted, brought to earth. After we got to your office
I went to the library and started writing this poem. I wanted to write a
dangerous poem, for a little danger is good for the soul, especially in this
safety-conscious land, an island of safety in a world crazy with violence,
and a little danger can slow down your life and give it some depth. Instead
it's turning into a small poem that someone might find some day and like,
not a dangerous poem in league with the world's great sonnets. There's no
reason to be embarrassed. No one will read it with any special understanding
for only the creator really knows his own creation, no one will say I know
who he's talking about, or what. This is a small poem outside time, a poem to
be discovered in a thousand years and perhaps enjoyed because of the sad
miracle of time, the sad sense of endless loss and wildly complex renewal,
because people will be sorry for us because we lived and now are dead.

But you were half an hour late and I was ten minutes early so I had forty
minutes to sit dreaming in the lobby of the Holiday Inn. You know how it is,
you're thinking about flowers and you get involved there in the lobby
in a long conversation with the bellhop about the wonderful silk flowers
on display on all the little tables. So at the information desk, naturally,
I chatted with the clerk about her flowers, the ones sitting on her counter.
The bird of paradise seemed real, so real the pollen stuck to my fingers.
There's a real flower in this bunch, I said, and she said they're all real,
and she looked at the bird of paradise and said she didn't care for it—
too shamelessly sexual I suppose. So I zipped into the candy store there
in the lobby and bought four Geneva violets, little chocolates with a candy
violet on the top of each and with a small yellow dot in each violet's centre.
When you finally arrived flushed and apologetic as Apollo, I gave you one
and I had one and after lunch I gave you the remaining two to take back to
the office with you, one for you and one for your secretary. Tell her it's
from the man with the nice voice, I said, and you kissed me on the nose. I
love the way you instinctively kiss me when I do or say something you think
is nice. It's been like this for millennia. Women turning apes into angels.

42. Invisibility

God is a predator we had to invent for lack of any serious predators
of our own: as if the owl were the fieldmouse's god or you your tropical
fish. Usually that which surrounds you ignores you even though you know
you are there, visible and anxious. But there are times when trees seem to
bloom at your approach, clouds form images of you in the sky, and the CN
Tower and the brown-skinned buildings along Spadina Road seem to know
all about you and even have complex silent dialogues with you about time.
They seem older than the Pyramids of Egypt and they treat you as if you
are just like them, existing everywhere at once, millennia old, beyond
time and eternity, ignorance and omniscience, importance and impotence.
The world knows nothing of this and goes on noisily without you and you
are mysteriously uncaring and you feel yourself dissolving into strange
invisibility and perfect felicity and you know that if the planet were to be
destroyed in a global nuclear firestorm you'd take it as a personal insult
of immense proportions but that would soon pass. You don't dwell on these
things, you, the CN Tower, the buildings along Spadina Road, you don't
bother clinging to such trivial concerns as the world. Things outside time
stream through you like the events of time but you are not outside time:
you'll eventually dissolve and reappear in other forms on other worlds. And
as the citizens of this wonderful city ran around screaming, their flesh on
fire and falling from their bones, you would simply lapse into anonymous
invisibility, and that which surrounds you, that which exists inside your
magnetic field, would also quietly disappear. But what would never disappear
is the core of your felicity, for when you cry all the angels hear you, all
the angels are you, and when you laugh or even as you breathe, for wherever
you stand a large X appears at your feet. It seems that you are always at a
mystical intersection, watching automobiles collide with giant trucks,
children crying endlessly, giant mindless owls swooping down on little
fieldmice trying to hide in the tall grass among serious armies of ants.

I am a sensitive man and always know when something is not quite right
in my heart or the hearts of those standing on any X on which I have
ever stood. An hour ago I felt a certain fundamental distress, as if my
heart had flown and my mind and body were standing at different
intersections, but now we are all together and surrounded by silence.

43. My Own True Nature

Opera recordings first became available in 1949 while animal imagery
began to enter my dreams in 1969. Two dreams were so strange I made
paintings of them: a wild eagle sitting on my head, a wild bull with its
head cradled in my arms. These are the things true lovers tell each other.
I had a conversation with a herd of cattle, I followed a cow as it swam
across Lake Ontario, I was transformed into a mournful lion trapped
at the bottom of a deep dark well. Dreams urge us to be compassionate,
animals don't dream, they are okay without them, they live in the moment,
they don't bother with dreams or clothing. Trees and flowers seldom dream.
But since this is a poem about talking dogs and barking men I must tell you
that last night I was walking along a country road in the Slocan Valley and a
well-groomed well-bred Scottish collie the size of a small horse joined me.
His chin touched my shoulder as we walked along. He asked where I was going,
I told him just down the road a bit and then I'm coming back, he eagerly
asked if he could trot along beside me and I said I'd be delighted. As we
walked he said he thought humans were crazy to be always trying to improve
the world, it only made things worse, and he said he thought Zen Buddhism
was an instrument intended to drive the entire non-Japanese world insane.

I was on the collie's back, and we were trying to swim a powerful river,
the other side invisible in the mist. Later I was talking to a strange man who
confessed that he was really a dog. He rolled up his sleeve and
showed me his canine fur. He was nervously smoking Black Cat Filters. He
wanted to splash in a rain puddle there on the road but felt trapped
in his human role. He said he was seven but he looked at least forty-nine.
He certainly smelled like a dog, but you wouldn't have noticed it
unless he mentioned it, and he did, and he also smelled like a man.
He had that special smell of canine consciousness: dim, wet with saliva,
something you can feel but not describe. Yet superimposed was a
distinct human odour: dry, distant, full of thought, repressed to the
point of insanity, uncomfortably clean, a creation of the human language
he'd learned to use too well. I liked him, felt sympathy for his plight
which was mine as well, but I felt I liked that collie better, if I may be
permitted to express my likes and dislikes. And I remembered that Ernest
Hemingway's wives were always complaining because he never bathed,
never changed his clothes, never shaved. Always smelled of blood and guts.
I used to wonder how he could have killed all those beautiful animals and now
I know! It was because he was one himself! And in today's paper there's a
story from Russia about an elephant with a thousand-word vocabulary.

44. Death Beds

On their death beds Hoshin said, "I come from brilliance and I return to
brilliance," and Saroyan said, "I know everyone has to die but I always
thought an exception would be made in my case." As for me, I'm seldom
competitive. On my death bed I'll just say goodbye and if you try to console
me by saying my poems will live forever I'll pretend to be overjoyed,
incredulous, or maybe I'll hit you (weakly) with my intravenous bottle.

It's a habit, a hobby, and I'm always torn between inventing and recording,
trying to maintain the belief as of the Virgin Birth that all this matters.
If one man told the truth about his life the world's wounds would heal.
In time we'll doubt such perfect love and friendship ever existed, or
become blind to it. We were yacking so much this morning you missed
your train and I felt guilty so despite your protests I rented a car to
drive you to Stratford and we yacked so much in the car we got lost in
Tweed or Elmira, you missed your important meeting, and we ended up
spending the afternoon on the spectacular beach at Port Franks, and the
waves kept making your string bikini fall off and we got all brown and
sentimental in the sun and fell in love again. It'll be February or maybe
May before you see your husband again and although I've never met him
I know he's a great man and I want him to know what a good babysitter
you've had and somehow I know you'll always remember me. If you
hear I'm lonely you'll be sad, not well and you'll be even sadder, and
when you're reunited with him and these days are over forever all that
happens to me I'll imagine you hearing about it and thinking about it,
quietly, sadly, strangely, in your sad, quiet and strange little heart.

45. Richard II

I went to see *Jaws 3-D* at the Tivoli in Kitchener and showed up at one
incognito in my Niagara Falls captain's cap and 3-D glasses. You thought
I'd given up and gone back to Toronto and it was as if we'd been cruelly
separated by tragic fate for at least a year instead of a mere afternoon.
Remember the coffee we ordered in the morning, how unpalatable it was?
You went down to your meeting and I left, wondering if your colleagues were
looking out the window and saying there's so-and-so, what a coincidence!
What's he doing here? But I knew you'd handle it with cool aplomb. I went
to the bank and the smoke shop downtown and somehow managed to lose
the keys to the rented car, but I got to the beach by one and spent a couple
of hours sunning and swimming alone. "Where's your better half?" said
the fat old guy who ran the ice-cream stand and parking lot. "You mean
she let you come to the beach alone with all this meat running around?"
And his wife was also surprised to see me alone. They were both leering.
She wanted to charge me to use the toilet so I said I'd piss in the water.

And I did. My writing has always been of the day, has always been an
attempt to capture the magic of my own true days. I am a sentimental
schmuck, and this another special poem for another special day. I drove
back from the beach slowly along the back roads and when I reached your
hotel there you were out front and the people had left only moments before.
The angels as always handle our affairs with intelligence and deep concern,
although I can't figure out why they wanted me to lose those keys. Downtown
we saw Walter before he saw us, he was walking along looking in store windows
and we said if he crosses the street that will mean the angels want us to
have a drink with him, and he did. It didn't take long for him to get the
picture. But he was sad, he missed his family, he was sweet, and when I
went to the john (no charge) he told you what a wonderful writer I was.
Later, after seeing *Richard II* at the Avon with Brian Bedford as Richard
and Cedric Smith as Bolingbroke, we drove slowly back to Toronto, like a
man and woman who have been married for years, our closeness perhaps
a factor of our knowledge that we'll soon be torn apart, perhaps forever.

46. Nipples

The angels speak to me but with no greater wisdom than the wisdom
I feel I should possess but don't. They say they want to play a greater
role in my life, and they don't like it when I try to argue with them.
"Don't coax me," I might suddenly say aloud, sitting by myself on the
train, other passengers nervously glancing my way. For the angels try
to railroad me into adopting more fruitful ways of handling this kind of
freedom, boundless, highly dangerous. They're like nervous parents whose
teenagers want to stay out after midnight, even want the family car. It's
all fairly banal. They don't want to see me chopped to pieces at an ordinary
level crossing. Immortals and mortals alike enjoy these mutual bonds of
slavery, chains of golden light, invisible umbilical cords of enlightened
desire. The angels tell me my life is not yet over, there is much renewal
coming, they know when to mail images of spring flowers into my scorched
vision, they want me to come to terms with them, they're obsessed with me.

My perfect friend, you have flown away again, this time to Madrid, and I
discover you within me, our indwelling, and my mind and body are going
through the normally inevitable process of learning to care deeply and
not to care simultaneously. When the hero puts the milk in the fridge,
don't mention it. It's a different story when he puts the cat in the fridge.
Or touches an ice cube to instinct's little feline nipples. I promise not to
drink myself into a coma and something always tugs me off the track just
before the midnight express roars by. This indwelling, this presence, this
perfect closeness, you say you've felt it all along, the angels say I tend
to underestimate you, but this is new to me, and fragile, this fearlessness
that accompanies the newborn knowledge that there is nothing to fear.
Nothing can separate true minds but fear of sentimentalism, not even your
sudden death or flight to Madrid. We will always be naked, drinking glasses
of milk, illuminated by the light of the open fridge, the cats at our feet.
It will always be an hour before feeding time in the cathouse at the Granby
Zoo, and I will always be watching the sailboats on Lake Ontario while you
stand there, on your head, on a sandy patch of the stone-covered beach.

47. The Robe of Your Intelligence

I have the impression the roar of trucks along Spadina Road is disturbing
the row of fig trees on my balcony. The stems of the flowers I send you are
rooted in the blood and guts of unknown ancestors. We're human and want
to destroy the witches and Incas of our lack of understanding. This summer
flags have become a big issue in small towns throughout the United States.
If you don't fly a flag your neighbours will spit on you in the all-night
convenience store, and maybe even call you a Commie. A man and woman
wrap their baby in a stars-and-stripes blanket and walk down Main Street,
they say the world has to end some day, who cares if it ends in a nuclear
war? Humanity is a soft word, mankind hard. One doesn't say have a little
mankind. Tomorrow is Hiroshima Day and we now know all those people
were deep-fried not to end the war which was already over but to scare
the Russians out of trying to take over Europe. The only freedom worth
fighting for is the freedom to love well or the freedom to fight yourself
in order to prepare yourself to take on the task of destroying the nations,
to liberate the freedom to love. You asked me not to write about you....

And I agreed, and I wrote nothing because anything I would have written
would have been about you. The newly liberated angel of our love sits
among my fig trees watching the traffic roar by. The angels have taken
an interest in me because my love for you has made me attractive and has
made my existence more noticeable in their inconceivable realm. And they
have come to me like smalltown cops keeping me up all night with their
bright lights and asking me uncomfortable questions, and so, of course,
forgive me, I told them of my promise and how that destroyed the sense of
freedom I need, safe conduct, the sense I can pass through borders like
angels through walls, free of the dreary necessities, and they said ask her
to withdraw her objections, and so I did. And you said without hesitation
all right I will, your transparent eyes glistening like little hearts, as if
the angels had prepared you for my request. So now I can write about you
but not in any way that would compromise you. For your intelligence
has entered my life like a gibbous moon and has awakened my own little
intelligence and given it a style and consistency it hitherto lacked. And I
understand how your intelligence robes you in soft white light and how
your intelligence is noticed before anything else, before your merely
physical beauty. You present it to me and encourage me to use it and I want
to use it sparingly and gently, like light, gracefully, like music, not as
one eats flesh but as one enjoys ordinary existence and the freedom to love.

48. Beer and Pizza

It's Hiroshima Day and in the heat I lug a load of empties to the beer store.
It's too hot to think. I wait for my thoughts but they do not come streaming
up, they never do when I wait for them. Even the bus is slow to come.
Civilization ended thirty-eight years ago today. That's a thought, but it
fails to convince. A skinny old drunk in a red shirt staggers under a load
of empties, crosses the gas station lot, drops one case, the empties roll
all over the lot, he yells out ah shit, people sit in their cars and watch and
smile, nobody wants to help him. I'd help him for sure but I've got two
cases of my own, full, to contend with. So I yell across the street at him:
Make two trips! But he's too drunk to hear me. All over the world people
are drinking beer and thinking about Hiroshima, how the survivors
immediately after the blast speculated calmly on what the cause had been.

Swamp gas. A few nights ago someone torched the women's bookstore,
hoping to get the abortion clinic above. But the store was gutted, the clinic
untouched. And last night Sandy Stone phoned to tell me to get down to the
store, the local coven was having a purification ceremony. I'd been watching
a television program about spiders and when she phoned they were showing
a mother spider who shortly after the birth of her babies redirects her own
digestive fluids to turn her body into mush for the cute little things, and
her heart and lungs keep operating as the babies devour her body. When I
got there the women were sitting in a large circle amid candles, incense,
and were coincidentally chanting a hymn to the Great Spider: "You are the
web, you are the weaver," and they passed around a magic glass heart from
hand to hand and each woman who held it had to say a word about what the
bookstore meant to her. Frankly the comments weren't that interesting,
they were valedictorian in tone, and everyone was too nervous to sound
sincere. I wanted to tell them about my fabulous spider coincidence,
but by the time the heart got to me somehow they'd started chanting
again so Sandy and I looked at each other and decided to go for pizza.

49. Yoko Ono

You know what it's like. A thousand thoughts are swirling in your brain
and a thousand feelings in your heart. Everything's so overwhelming you
couldn't bother to put thyme in your scrambled eggs this morning. Sadness
is a grey sea in all directions, and a grey sky over it in all directions, and
it's all yours. You bought a new coat, you quit smoking, and you're so busy
you scarcely noticed it's the first day of the new year. Canadian winter: it's
so cold your nose froze and there's an icicle on your bicycle. Imagine! John
Lennon is dead and I'm alive. I told you as we fell asleep that when I awoke
you'd be gone and you were. You'll never return. Too problematic. I made
a pot of coffee and sat down and wrote a song, then phoned Yoko Ono and
sang it to her. She was nice. Put on my new coat, went out and found Walter
shivering on the corner, sad because his marriage was over but he says
at least I'm out of all that domestic pressure. He says he had a dream: he
dreamt he was an ancient bearded Blakean prophet standing chest-deep
in a frigid lake for thirteen hours each day in a sad mythical kingdom
high above the arctic, an adult's revision of what Santa Claus' North Pole
was really like, no elves, just the prophet and his childless wife sitting in
their house on the shore of the frigid lake. She was considering leaving
him, it was no good for her at all. The prophet had a rare nervous condition
that he felt could only be controlled by subjecting himself to such frigid
agony for thirteen hours every day. It made sense. That was his fate,
he was enlightened enough to know it, you can't pretend you're the same as
everyone else, you have to become a little mad to prevent yourself from
becoming absolutely mad. Your fate encompasses vast unknown truths.

So anyway, you are halfway to where you go when you leave me and I am
where I always am, a drop suspended in the grey sea of sadness you begin
to notice when you get tired of being tragic all the time. You said you
needed a clean break and a stream of soapy water squirted out of my eye.
You left silently before I awoke and flew to Maui or somewhere. I took
the train to Central Park and stared up at Yoko Ono's window. She noticed
and sent a note down. The note said: When you see the sadness of life
everywhere you look you're halfway there. I said by now she's probably
all the way there, and I'm here, chestdeep in an arctic lake. You know me,
I always have to say what I think, my life has been a parody of honesty.
Not that what I think is always what I think. For instance, I told her my
poems would continue to be read long after John Lennon is forgotten,
and she said you don't really think that, and I said I did think that but
now I don't. So I spent a week talking to elephants in the zoo and when
I returned you were back in town after lying on the beach all week having
nonstop imaginary conversations with me. We made solemn vows to continue
in this same way forever: the warmth when two frigid lakes come together,
the thunder when two immense grey sadnesses wash up against each other.

50. God Save the Queen!

The angels know little about the irony with which we view our agony. It's inexpressible, even to them. Let's face it, there's no end to poetry. Just when the world is dead and you feel it's all been said you hear of a man who cut off his penis on being rejected by his lover. And in your dream you're holding three cut penises in the palm of your hand, inspecting them for signs of rot, wondering if you should store them in the cooler for future reattachment. You begin to feel, with sadness, as sad as you ever get in mere dreams, a fourth growing, and you know it too will end up being severed. If each day you write a line of poetry and keep from each line all trace of irony will something worthwhile come from all your agony?

I remember the taste of chocolate milkshakes at the Co-op Dairy in the east end of Hamilton on Sunday afternoons in 1952, spending the money I was supposed to have put in the Sunday school collection plate, and the kindergarten teacher taking us to the blacksmith's shop behind the dairy, or taking us to Gage Park in October to collect fall leaves for waxing. I remember the look of anguish on my brother's face when, aged seven, he saw me standing in the shower and said, "Oh no, not hair there!" Now he's almost forty and I lie here smiling in the dark, my hands behind my head, wondering what it would have been like to have been John Stubbs, the printer, who printed something Queen Elizabeth didn't like and so she had his right hand chopped off, and with blood spurting from the fresh stump he raised his hat with his left hand and shouted God Save the Queen!

51. Zen

There are no other worlds, everything-all-at-once is right here, this
is one stage that doesn't need props or prompts, the only stagehands
are the angels in your dreams and they are merely reminders of the normally
hidden perfection of the friends who daily surround you, the ones you sadly
and mistakenly see as tragic, they are otherwise so dangerously difficult
to see, unless in the kitchen memos of our dreams. Zen is having the
courage to become enlightened in the guts. Who is this person I am
trying to impress with these flabby imitations of the Sonnets, the
Sermon on the Mount, the Diamond Sutra—for the purest and most
angelic reasons of course? Some Platonic friend or other. Each of us
is everything and everyone, everything is perfect, always has been,
coldly, obviously, heartlessly. Who has suffered enough but Jesus? That
poet who hid his name in the King James version of Psalm 46, the poet
in Elizabethan nakedness who appears in our dreams nailed to a cross.
It didn't occur to him to try to avoid the implications of what he was
saying and not saying simultaneously with his sad eyes and thorny sonnets.
There is no middle ground: we either perish or become resurrected, and the
nails of our affections are composed of our intolerance for mediocrity.

Naturally I want to know if you know what I feel is obviously ambiguous.
Are the things we never say to each other too obvious to bother saying
or are they things that are not said or even seen by anyone who doesn't
have the courage to be enlightened in the guts? Why aren't we as free
from desire as we'd ever desire to be? I thought we would have been
burned out long ago but instead we seem to be on the verge of burning
more and more brightly. Everyone loves you, everyone loves me, but you
don't love that many people and neither do I. You're a spring of clear
spirit and I'm a wandering angel of mercy in drag, spreading joy everywhere
all at once, mindlessly, aimlessly, which doesn't take much courage. Who knows
how far these little poems will travel? And think of the courage it would
take to write something that would always be true? No courage at all!

52. Caucasian Shower

A sudden silent gap in traffic and the single lazy early-morning wail
of a cat. The city is a jail. I don't want to check my mail, there'll be
nothing there from you. We've failed. I sit here thinking about myself,
which is to say about you. It'd be nice if you were here but it's okay
that you're not. Any time I want I can amuse myself by thinking of you
and imagining you here. Or me there. Or both of us anywhere, suddenly
looking at each other silent with pleasure. For I'm a man of passion but
no sorrow, happily and forever isolated from the people of this smug
provincial city and their predictable lusts. My friends, whom I seldom
see, accuse me of being self-obsessed. I roll my eyes and say Toulouse
Lautrec had short legs. Time to be selfless when you're old, full of
sorrow and no passion. How could they be so stupid not to see I've simply
grown tired of pretending to be pure? I look in the mirror and am truly
astonished by my sudden radiant youthfulness. So this is what being alone
does to you? Almost as good as heavy drinking! I sleep contentedly afloat
in a river of transparent blood, a small fast stream flowing through the
guts of an undiscovered continent: where will it take me and how soon? At
the next bend I could be awakened, captured, tortured. Furthermore, why
did I, notorious for being cheerful in the morning (intimates say I'm a nice
guy except for my singing in the shower), wake up this morning thinking
about lampshades of human skin? I look at my own lonely belly with its
sad single eye that never closes, not even when smothered in overcoats,
the eye that says I don't wanna be no lampshade and I don't wanna turn
anyone else into lampshades. Self-obsession! I wasn't even dreaming
about lampshades. I dreamt about a very nice man who arrested me for
smuggling fresh orange juice into frozen Canada, I told him I didn't mind
paying a fine or even going to jail but I'd love to be able to hang on to my
juice, if possible. He was a handsome man but when he spoke his tongue
hung out and looked like a frozen pork chop. It was rather distracting
and frankly disgusting. It ruined his appearance totally. He looked like one
of those men who assassinated Lorca for being gay but he let me keep my
juice and it turned out he knew my friend Walter whom he immediately began
analysing, saying Walter's interest in demon possession was becoming a
scandal. It makes the English department look bad. Let's shoot him, I said.

Of course! That's why I was dreaming about lampshades! You can't allow
yourself to dream about lampshades of human skin, you'd be so horrified
it'd wake you up. So you have to dream about orange juice. Orange juice
symbolizes the demonology of making lampshades from human skin. That's
the way the mind works! You're not dealing with naïveté here! I'm no
dummy when it comes to symbolism. Whenever you think of orange juice,
it's a psychological cover for images from our collective storehouse
of unbearable horror. And then it all made sense: at lunch yesterday Walter,
who joined the Greek Church when he found out they believed in possession,
quoted C. G. Jung as having said in an interview in 1945 that yes he believed
in demons, and furthermore (Walter is a serious Baudelaire specialist) Jung
stated: "I know there are demons—just as sure as there's a Buchenvald."

53. Ocean of Sadness

Oh, I'm a man of passion but no sorrow. I observe from happy distances
the dark springs of sadness springing darkly in my breast. They sprang
into my dreams last night. I was a kid growing up in a vast artificial
satellite at war with dozens of other artificial satellites we'd been told
contained non-human beings from other galaxies. As I grew up I began
to realize we'd been lied to, the three million people in the satellite
we'd just clobbered were human beings just like us, from Earth, from
Italy actually. How they must have carried on during the last few hours
when they knew they'd been hit, the main system was beyond repair,
there wouldn't be a survivor. Nothing could be compared to such sorrow!
Happiness is an illusion, I told a young friend this afternoon. Then sorrow
is as well, he replied. I hope he never has to open his eyes; no, that's a
lie, it's his universe, he can look at it any way he wants, it doesn't matter,
but it's ultimately, I believe, worth it, to open the eyes, to see yourself
chuckling in a little boat on a vast ocean of sadness, the great spirit that
contains all our little I's like a library in which every book contains only
the letter I in every conceivable font, with old ones being deleted and
hitherto unimaginable new ones being inserted every moment. Nothing is
real but sadness, everything you can think of is composed of nothing but.
Even the tiny neutron is composed of billions of units of sadness. God
created the universe because he was sad. This will be on the (final) exam.

Everything is true of everybody, when you think of it. Everybody's in
heaven right now, and the universe is an ocean of sadness with no shore.
My friends never call, they think I've become terrifyingly vain, simply
because I like to talk about the shock of looking in the mirror and seeing
the sagging of the jowls and the sprigs of tough hair cascading from
nostrils and ears, just because I happen to think I'm the only interesting
person around except for the dark lady I'm trying to impress with these
poems. This is truly ridiculous, the way poets become involved in so many
strange situations. It's fate. You of all people know how stupid I am and
how I continually try to prove it. You wouldn't have it any other way.
I don't want to disappoint you so I won't say a thing. One values a poet to
the extent he or she is able to speak plainly of that which lies deep within
the global heart. With me this is a belief, a brilliance, a sad drowning in
sadness, a vacuum through which vanity winks like an extinct star.

54. The Sacrifice of Desire

I passed the night in the all-night doughnut shop at the corner of Bloor and
Walmer playing Pacman with the richest man in the world, his Rolls parked
around the corner, his chauffeur watching us play and lighting our cigars.
He won a game and told me he was the richest man in the world and I said
that's quite a coincidence, I'm the greatest poet in the world. He said that
may be my opinion but others would disagree. I agreed. He didn't ask to see
my poems even though they were all there in my Shoppers Drug Mart plastic
bag. If he'd liked them he could have become my lifetime patron, I could have
told the Canada Council where to go. So he went in his Gucci briefcase and
pulled out a sheaf of papers that proved to my satisfaction that yes indeed
he was the richest man in the world. Without identifying him (a promise)
I can say he was vitally interested in the arts of war and was shamelessly
delighted with the way things were going in Laos, Lebanon and Libya
and was getting quite excited about certain events in Central America.
I was sympathetic (as always) but told him that under the circumstances
it would be impossible for me to accept his patronage. He said he wasn't
offering it. Amazing how equal we were Pacmanskillwise, he'd win one
and I'd win the next, which was nice, and made the night go quickly. We
didn't argue, but when I told him it bothered me that Toronto's new concert
hall was called Roy Thompson Hall rather than Glenn Gould Hall he said I
was being silly, making money was as much of an art as playing the piano,
and Roy was as deserving of immortal fame as Glenn. You should start a
campaign, he said, to get the new domed stadium named after Glenn Gould.

So I can state with authority that nobody's satisfied, not even the richest
man in the world. Actually, he was full of a yucky sort of sentimental envy
of the poor even though he refused to give a quarter to a deaf mute who
didn't have the price of a coffee. We shouldn't encourage them, he said.
Come to think of it I paid for all my Pacman games and most of his as well.
But this poem is about satisfaction and its sadly short supply in the world.
I want to tell you something and I won't be satisfied till I do. I think I've
discovered the secret of being totally satisfied in life. You have to let your
desires cancel each other out. No one's seriously suggesting desire can be
literally sacrificed like a virgin at midnight under a full moon atop the
pyramid of I-want-you-and-don't-want-you-at-the-same-time. No, you have
to play your desires against each other like a rich man and a poet playing Pacman.
There's nothing wrong with being continually dissatisfied except it's so
common. To get rid of one desire develop a strong counter-desire, one that
can only be fulfilled in the absence of fulfilment of the first desire and
for which you would have no desire if the first desire could be fulfilled.
Finally, I was joking earlier, I know I'm not the greatest poet in the world,
maybe not even in the top three, but you have to admit there are important
messages in my stuff and my weird sense of humour is worth supporting,
either by the Canada Council or by some rich person who's made his money
in some relatively moral way, or maybe eventually by my r!o!y!a!l!t!i!e!s!...

55. Woman Descending from a Train

Sometimes when I dream of other worlds I dream in colours that do not
exist on earth and I do not try to name them, they are not beautiful,
they nauseate me, terrify me, enrage me, depress me, and cause me to
forget the simplest things, just as certain odours in waking life can
turn an environmentally sensitive person into a pain-wracked paranoid.
Sometimes I feel that you and I have together undreamingly uncovered
a hitherto undetected tunnel that leads us down into a virgin planet of
pleasures that do not exist on earth and I do not try to name them but
they certainly do not nauseate me. Sometimes I feel capable of perceiving
love's mathematical equations and a basic rockbottom universal harmony.
Sometimes I feel we are at home only under the earth's snowy surface
and the truest transparent colours are escaping into the open air and are
charging the planet with the purest transparent realizations of the
warmth and perfection of which it is composed. Sometimes I feel I've
become transparent, afloat on the ocean of milk you've secreted for me,
and sometimes I feel I'll continue floating along like this long after
you have gone your own incomprehensibly dismal (to me) way, for now
your life is about to swing away from mine, most probably forever.

Our love has led us into caverns of mythical treasure under the surfaces of
daily dullness. We have awakened each other. The world gave birth to you,
and the thought of it having done so electrifies me with sparks and flames.

56. My Secret Ambition

Strange, silent, anonymous, unmoving but powerful enough to awaken
the slumbering heart, capable of being viewed from every window,
from a million different angles through the centuries, like Fujiyama,
the Standing Stones at Callinish, Glastonbury Tor. That is what I shall
dedicate what is left of my pleasant little life (this kind of ambition is
not entirely unattractive, even in a person of middle age) to building,
total devotion to that and nothing else. I am sitting on the train. I have
eyes, ears, and so on, one of a strange and powerful species. My name
is merely the mortar for these rough-hewn blocks and will serve merely
to stress the impersonality of this strange work, the purity of its
coming into being. How could I have forgotten that everything is truly
anonymous? The blossoms on the cherry branch, the central fire of the
hungriest heart, the most insanely monomaniacal ego are shot through
with purest anonymity, like earthworms, herds of cows, all of history.
Everything is automatic, mechanical, an energetic swarm of bees, all
composed of billions of electrons, photons, everything is an image
on God's screen. And the great suffering ego is God's biggest joke.
Listen and you'll hear him roaring with silent laughter. Everything
is pure like air. Everything is sweet as our love. Peace is everywhere.

After the knife fight in Borges' "The Meeting," the final words of the
defeated man: "How strange! All this is like a dream." And then he died.
A certain man aroused a certain jealousy in me. I said he was an idiot but
of course I was the idiot. No knife fight. Apologies to both of you. It's
time now for me to give up the idea of perfection we shared. It's time
now for me to return to my essential nothingness, a nothingness that
generates small dreams and poems as expressions of eternal silence.

57. Accordion Solo

That's where I thought you were, I'd quietly say as I sat on my mother's
lap, she'd be reading to me, I'd ask her where she was, she'd point to a
word, and then I'd fall off her lap and learn something about the
unreliability of intelligence and imagination. We have this funny little
squeezebox called the lungs and out of empty air words emerge. You can
arrange them on a page in lines and call it poetry. Poetry is potency,
someone spraybombed on the wall up the street and suddenly you see
language coming in long snake-like sexual corridors bordered with crystal
walls and reflecting mirrors. Life on earth is a miracle happening only
once in all of space and time. Language is the source of consciousness, for
language reminds one inevitably of silence and to be conscious is to be
conscious of silence before everything. Do you talk in your sleep and if so
do you listen? My mother once told me she heard me say in my sleep: "I
don't talk in my sleep." And I heard her say: "I've got my own religion: I'm a
lover of nature." But she denied it, said I must have made that up, read that
somewhere, she belonged to the United Church. And I would fantasize for
hours about being crucified, taken down from the cross, and my mother
would take me in her arms and stare into my dead face with cosmic woe.
I'm glad English is my mother tongue because it was also Shakespeare's
and Shakespeare always reminded me of Christ although Shakespeare
is a tad easier to understand and he did his bit, and suffered. Sent the
same poem to at least two different women, wrote as easily as he
breathed and thought, lived passionately and maybe even mythologically.

Here it is five in the morning again, me too happy to sleep, so I lie here
watching the sky lighten and listening to the gradual increase in traffic.
It was wonderful of you to visit, and I only wish you could have arrived
earlier and stayed longer. There's always a big fat angel almost visible
above our heads when we're together. The birds of course are singing.
Thanks for letting me read so many of my favourite sonnets to you,
I've never read them better and probably never will. At any rate it gave us
the chance to speak with warm passion about the difference between
friendship and love and of the various elements of each in the other.
Friendship is no less a mystery than love, to quote Borges, and whose soul
would remain unstirred by the perfect purity and intensity of the lovely
friendship Will bore for the young W.H.? Who can love so purely today?
Maybe we can. Let's try. Let's have a friendship that'll set the clock
back four centuries. I don't care if we can't be together as long as
we're together. Besides, the spell of a night with you will never die.

58. The Two of Cups

Everything is lacklustre without you. I really think I can't live
without you, has anyone ever tried that old cliché on you before?
I had all these ideas for a sweet little poem then thought what the
hell why not just write something human? I'm a great fan of Malcolm
Lowry's little poems as blistering as yellow clouds of mustard gas.
So I just got back from the Sticky Wicket where I sat at the bar in my
raincoat and thought about my friend Walter's poem about Humphrey
Bogart six months after the final scene in Casablanca pounding himself
on the head with a gin bottle and saying stupid bastard over and over.
I sat there drinking tequila (I prefer mescal but it has the effect of
causing me to wake up bruised and naked at the bottom of a fire escape in
Hamilton, Ontario, no matter where I started drinking it). Strangely,
all the way home I thought about you, then checked my book and said
no wonder, I haven't seen you since April 23, haven't heard your voice
since May 23, and here it is June 23. My friends have lost their spark,
their charm. Of late I'm incapable of having a spirited discourse with
anyone. I wanted to do and say all the noble things, like Bogie, but when
it came time to do them it felt as if that would be fake nobility, true
nobility lies in saying what you think and feel. A woman picked me up
in the bar a couple of nights ago. She took me home and got into this
horrible silk jumpsuit, drenched herself in perfume and wanted me
to look into her eyes. The deal's off, I said. As for my eyes they're so
sad I've taken to wearing sunglasses night and day. No one should
have to look at eyes as sad as my redrimmed little heartbreakers.

So I went to see Samantha and the Hermit came up next to the Two of Cups.
She got excited and said this is the highest form of love imaginable,
this is a true marriage of mind and heart and body, this woman is not
doing herself any favours by staying away from you, she's very much
in love with you there's no doubt about that, and she said with unearthly
authority: *She'll never find another man like you.* Play it again,
Sam. So I'm living inside myself where the moon always shines on the
palms and pines and there's never anybody home but me. Come with me,
we'll take a dog team across Antarctica, we'll make love in every major
city in the world except Paris and Rome (they don't need it). And if you
can't come send someone who looks, breathes, speaks and tastes like you.

59. Trying to Figure It Out

I hated him in grade 5 but now he was all grown up. He said he had
four children and the whole family waterskied in the summer and
snowmobiled in the winter. I said I hated you in grade 5 and I can't
figure out why but I still hate you. He stared at me and I stared back.
But we kept on chatting, waiting in line at the Canadian Tire checkout
counter. I told him I've changed, I now enjoy drinking hard liquor
from morning to night and becoming overfriendly on the street with
Oriental women with broken umbrellas and I'm obsessed with writing
little poems that everyone would understand all too well if they were
to read them. He stared some more. That night when I closed my eyes
I saw four little revolving windmills: red, yellow, blue and green, and
later dreamt the kid I hated in grade 5 had died and come back to life.
I saw him with his widow. He said when he died his spirit roamed all
over the world until he found his earthly double, same red hair, same
little round nose, and he pushed that man's spirit out of his body and
entered with his own, then made his way back to his widow, who
didn't look all that pleased. I told him I couldn't see any difference.

I slept late and lightly dreamt you and I were lying in bed together
watching a movie on TV. I was sleeping so lightly I knew I was sleeping
and thought you were really there but when I looked at the TV again it
wasn't on and I thought the movie had been a dream but you were really
there, for I clearly felt your warm breasts and your warm breath shifting,
but when I turned to look you weren't there and I became awake and full
of sadness. Decided I had to do something but there was nothing to do but
try to change my feelings, so I had a good long pull on my bedside bottle
and got out my old diaries, wondering where I went wrong. I know anyone
who reads these poems will shudder and think I'm nuts, but that's fine,
I want the reader to know he's not alone under his sane Paris fashions.
On the surface my life is an unbelievable mess and requires incredible
balance to keep me from plunging into absolute despair and suicide.
But inside, in my naked spacious heart, I feel absolutely wonderful!

60. My Old Diaries

What gets me is the amazing clarity yet totally unconscious inability
to understand people. In my twenties I was stupid as birthday balloons
with happy faces, persevering, loyal, loving, no battle with myself or
guilt. Now the world is fresh and innocent and I am not. I knew about
paradox but it scared me and now it saves me. I can't prove that two and
two ain't four but we see it all around us, right? I steel myself to
read the poems I wrote in those days and my daily jottings and I have
no desire to rewrite history but simply to assimilate my past, to figure
out where all this guilt and pain are coming from. Books about UFOs
frightened me. Did I really think that Janice having the flu and Sid
having a headache on Jan. 14/69 would be of any interest to me in the
future? And why did I record the weather every day? Absolutely no
recollection that on Jan. 11 that year I watched an old Fred Astaire
movie in which someone says: "You're a success, you pursue pleasure
and find it everywhere, wherever you go, but I've locked myself in the
woods for the past twenty years trying to write like Thoreau and failed."
How could I ever have imagined myself as a poet, it was obviously
a factor of people wanting me to be a poet: Stan, Michael, Victor,
for I had no language except that which people could pull out of me.
I don't remember having a sore arm but it says here I was on heavy
doses of codeine for it for three weeks. It's nice though to be reminded
that I was a passionate amateur gardener and took great pride in my
dahlias and roses. I don't remember going to the lawyer on Sept. 3
to make a will. Picasso would never make a will because he thought that
if he did he'd die the next day for sure. But I do remember clearly seeing
a flying saucer that night flying south above Kenilworth Avenue
and there's no mention of it. My daughter wanted to be a fish for
Halloween and looked down a hole in the grass, and said she could see
a bunny down there, and wrote a poem that went: "Birds can fly,
butterflies can fly, why can't I?" She thought cars were alive.

Don't be afraid to sentimentalize, says Gabriel Marquez, and don't
let yourself be cowed by the intellectuals. Just bite into all the apples
and summon up all the fire you can. You pay for it, but what the hell.

61. Peace

Joan, you won't remember this, but twenty years ago today you took my car out
for a spin with no oil and burnt out the engine. Cost me two hundred bucks.
It's all right here in my diary, though I can't remember what car it was.
And an apartment building exploded in Greenland killing all the tenants.
We went to see *I Am Curious (Yellow)* and you said it wasn't boring like
all the critics said it was. I was making $178 a week as a night proofreader
and the editor offered me a raise to $185 if I'd become a police reporter.
We had to borrow ten bucks from your mom for groceries. I took the job.
Jack Wilson died of stomach cancer. He was ten years older than we
were then and ten years younger than we are now. (Mocking chronology.)
Two days before his death I went to visit him in the hospital and read him
some poems from Al Purdy's new book. He liked them and said if he had his
life to relive he'd be a poet. Remember how funny he was? And his
pencil-thin moustache? He managed a little toy store at the shopping
centre where the racetrack used to be. I took Jennifer to John Boyle's
studio in St. Catharines and we bought his "Spanish Heel" (which I
still have) on credit. When I missed a payment or two he sent some Hell's
Angel guy to call on us. For Father's Day you bought me a pair of brown
Wellingtons. For your birthday I bought you a silver tray. In the middle
of the night I'd wake up feeling you'd been having a sneak affair with
Victor Coleman! I was annoyed with myself for having told Glenn Sinclair
my salary! My first byline appeared in the paper and my mom said to her
friends, Did you notice it was my son who wrote the story? I asked Alison
how she got so funny and she said she learned it from Jennifer. You asked
Alison why she was giggling so much and she said, "Because I got a big
joy." Dick Sherman wanted you to pose in the nude but you were too
much of a prude and now he's dead and can look at you in the nude
any time he wants from the spirit plane. Lots of entries about your
early interest in Bliss symbols and handicapped children, your weekly
visits to the hairdresser, your hour-long phone calls with your mother
three times a day, your being annoyed because I was late coming home,
and a beautifully loving note you put in my diary for me to see the next
day or the next decade, in which you call me "the world's best husband."

I tried. What gets me is the energy! We were always so furiously busy!
Everything's so peaceful now, isn't it? We have our loneliness, pain
and guilt that will never entirely disappear, but there's so much peace!

62. Cadillac Moon

We've just spent a day of piracy together. We met by innocent design
in Belleville, I drove you back to Montreal in a new Cadillac and that was
that, we don't know when we'll meet again but we know we will. When
we feel anger and have no one to direct it against we naturally have to
invent enemies. I feel anger, resentment, bitterness but it's no one's
fault, we're trapped in a kind of circumstantial cruelty that seems
merely funny when looked at with any kind of perspective but it requires
too much effort to maintain any kind of perspective at times like this.
All I can do is try not to lie to myself and try not to lie to you. Wasted
lovely brutal days and nights, I want to spend some time on the blue
foaming beaches of Lake Huron and take in all the plays at Stratford
and Niagara but I don't want to go by myself and no one else will do
and so I stay at home. On the old brown wall outside the Bloor Street
United Church someone has spraybombed in white paint GOD WAS HERE,
and I tell you about it silently in my mind. The next day I see someone
has been trying to erase the words and actually has managed to erase
the G and so I tell you about that in my mind as well. The next day
the whole slogan has been professionally removed, with money from
the United Church Graffiti Removal Slush Fund I suppose and I go to the
Viva Zapata and have three Carta Blancas and a huge plate of macho nachos
and I tell you that in my mind as well. Such grotesque sentimentality!
But if you were free we'd get Stan to lend us his Porsche and we'd spend
a week exploring the Kawarthas and Muskokas, swimming and getting burned.

So in my dreams I evoke people to hate, to blame for my terrible plight.
Two men I used to know and hate, Englishmen who thought Adolf Hitler
had received bad press, you know the type, appeared but it didn't work,
I couldn't hate them because in real life they had recently died, of cancer,
and I felt sorry for them. But one of my best friends in real life went by
in the dream, and I overheard him telling his colleagues that my poetry
is no longer worth reading! And I was so irrationally bitter and resentful
I yelled out after him: "Remember when we used to be lovers, Walter?"

63. An Artist's Prayer

The close of an autumn day brings with it an infinite number of
delicious sensations, vague for sure but their vagueness doesn't
lessen their number, their intensity or their ability to pierce you with
sorrow, for there is no point sharper or more sorrowful than that
of the infinite. Sounds French to me, says Professor Davey, looking
over my shoulder. The French, he says, have problems with the concrete
object, are not sure it really exists, and if they are sure they're not sure
it's a good thing it does exist. Thanks, Frank. But what magnificent delight
comes from drowning your gaze in the sky's immensity, and the sea's!
Such incomparable chastity, solitude, silence. My irremediable little life
is imitated by the little sailboat quivering on the horizon and by the
monotonous melody of the waves, for all these things think through me
although I shouldn't say "me," for in the grandeur of meditation I
quickly lose my ego. These things think, I say, but they think as music
thinks, as beautiful paintings think, without quibbling, like a poet's
thinking. But all of this thinking, however spontaneous and natural,
and whether it springs from me or the sky and the sea surrounding me,
soon becomes too intense, this intense sensual delight feeds so ravenously
on human energy the nerves begin producing shrill and woeful vibrations.

So everything turns around, and now the profundity and clarity of the sky
exasperates and dismays me, and I am revolted by the insensibility and
spectacular immutability of the sea. Beauty forces us to make a cruel
choice: we can either flee or suffer it all our lives. A poet must suffer the
frustration of seeing nature as his lifelong rival, and for his entire life he
never for a moment thinks that he could possibly win in the end. And the
study of beauty is a duel with swords and pistols, an unequal duel in every
way, for only the artist cries with fear, only the artist loses, endlessly.
Oh pitiless enchantress, nature, leave me in peace, stop tempting my
desires, my dignity, and leave me to go blindly through my life alone.

After Baudelaire's "Le Confiteor de l'artiste."

64. The Spirit of Toronto

New Year's Eve in Toronto the great, the official ecstasy of it all, the
provincial smugness crawling with greed and despair, a chaos of slush
and snow, thousands of cars smashing into each other as they race to
make the only green light in the entire universe, the city sparkling
with tinsel and little wrapped gifts for the kiddies. All this is enough
to trouble the mind of the most determined recluse. Further, my brain
is all gummed up with a recent bubble of a dream in which my poor old
mother appeared, but I think she really represented you. You know how
lovers tend to want to mother the beloved, to strive to give the beloved
a love as pure, undying and selfless as a mother's. Well, we were on a ship
sailing in the Baltic night, heading east towards Mother Russia, and another
ship was approaching from the east, an unfriendly ship which would have
fired on us and taken us captive but it apparently hadn't detected us yet.
It was imperative that we abandon ship and as I was packing my bags the
lights went out. Mother and I were the only ones aboard, and mother was
the captain, it appeared. And I as a grown man felt terribly embarrassed
to have to ask mother this: "Mother, why have all the lights gone out?"

So I awoke and stumbled out into the street in the middle of all this chaos
and official ecstasy, automatons with fur hats, amateur night for drunks,
and I began thinking about the suppressed rage and murder in the air,
all through the city, all through the country, how horrible if we could
kill anyone we wanted without fear of punishment! And the politeness
we are famous for is such a sham! But at the corner of Bloor and Yonge
a Spanish bull came ambling by, what a wonderful surprise, it must have
escaped from the back of a truck bound for the exhibition grounds or the
dogfood plant or some china shop, and as the creature came around the corner
a silly-looking Rosedale fop came out of nowhere, he was dressed in
patent-leather shoes, a necktie tight as a noose, a white silk scarf
and gloves, and he was imprisoned in an elegant wolverine overcoat.
He bowed ceremoniously before the poor animal and said to it: "I wish
you a good and prosperous new year, my friend," then returned to his
admiring companions with a conceited air, as if asking them to add their
approval to the smug and supercilious air of his banal contentment. I was
pleased to note the old warrior hadn't even noticed this joker, and began
trotting west on Bloor with some street urchins running insanely beside him.
This little scene will stay with me, for this flatulent fur-coated imbecile
appeared to have concentrated within himself the entire spirit of Toronto.

After Baudelaire's "Un Plaisant."

65. Heading towards Buchenvald

I am sitting here alone (as always) in my room staring at the wall and I notice
the room has become charged with something truly spiritual, the air is no
longer stagnant and gloomy but tinged lightly with subtle rays of rose and
blue coming from God knows where. It's as if my very soul is taking a bath
in rare waters luxuriously scented with delicate drops of regret and desire,
it's as if I've fallen asleep (although I'm wide awake) and am dreaming of
some subtle ritual of sensual delight being enacted during a lunar eclipse.
There is something of Picasso's spirit in the air, though he won't even be
born for a couple of decades: the furnishings have become elongated as if
again in a dream they've become endowed with a strange somnambulism,
like vegetables or maybe even minerals they speak a silent language, the
language of flowers, of autumnal skies, of radiantly lifeless planets. Yes,
and there are no pictures on the walls, no artistic abominations, which
naturally adds to this mood of deliciously obscure harmony, for what we
call art is blasphemy when placed beside pure dream and unanalyzable
spiritual impressions of whatever dimension or degree of intensity.
Everything here is endowed with sufficient clarity of its own and requires
little or nothing of human interpretation, here where my slumbering
spirit is nursed like a hothouse geranium, and an uncategorizably subtle
and exquisite perfume swims through the somewhat humid light. Hold on!
Hey, I'm not alone! My Queen of Dreams is here, reclining on the bed!
Where did she come from, how did she get here, what magic power has
placed her on this throne of sensuality? Who cares? She's here! Hurray!
And her horrendously malevolent eyes flash across the darkness, those
black stars that command such admiration and devour the gaze of anyone
impudent enough to contemplate them. Ah, such beatitude! Time itself
stops, and it is eternity which rules, an eternity of sensual delight!

But suddenly there's a terrible knock on the door and it's as if I've been
smacked in the gut with a pickaxe. It's some process-server who's come
to torment me in the name of the law, or it's a woman I made the mistake
of sleeping with once and she's sobbing miserably, or it's the copyboy from
the daily rag clamoring for the next instalment of my tedious critiques.
And all that magic disappears. And I remember with horror that this room
is my own, this slum, this abode of eternal boredom, and these are my sad
windows where raindrops have traced their little trails in the soot, sad
stacks of manuscripts in various stages of impossible completion, sad
calendars with particularly ominous dates encircled with black grease.
As for the perfume, all I can smell now is stale tobacco mixed with some
indefinable and nauseating mold, rancid and desolate. The only thing with
the capacity to make me smile in this narrow room is my dwindling stash
of opium but even its lovely caresses are typically full of betrayals.
The brutal dictatorship of Time has been reinstated and I am jabbed
with prongs, as if this room were a boxcar heading towards Buchenvald.

After Baudelaire's "La Chambre double."

66. Monkey on My Back

Under a vast grey sky in the nineteenth century, on a great dust-swept
plain, without roads, without grass, without a thistle or even a nettle,
I met a bunch of unearthly weirdos walking along with bowed heads. God,
the things I see! Right away I knew this would become transformed into
a great poem, and perhaps eventually would become my most famous! For
each of these guys was carrying on his back an enormous and ferocious
monkey, heavier than a sack of coal, heavier than all that stuff a Roman
soldier had to carry everywhere he went. And each monkey held on to its
poor host with all the force of its strong and supple muscles, each glued
itself to the man's chest with two huge clawed hands, and each held its
moronic face over the man's head like one of those horrible helmets worn
by ancient soldiers who hoped thereby to terrorize the enemy. So I went up
to one of these men and asked him quietly where he was going with such an
unusual burden. He looked at me as if I were nuts, said he didn't know what
the hell I was talking about, and he kept on walking, didn't miss a step, and
I could get nowhere with the others either. They just looked at me dumbly.
But it was evident they were going somewhere since they had such a great
aversion to stopping. And so they kept on walking. And I watching.

And thinking. It was curious that not one of these travellers seemed to be
bothered in the slightest by the ferocious beast hanging from his neck
and glued to his back. It seemed that each one thought of his beast as
being part of himself. They looked tired and their faces were serious
but there was no despair, and under the grey and depressing dome of the
sky their feet kept trudging through the dust of a country more desolate
than heaven, walking with the horrendous resignation of those condemned
to continue endlessly to hope. And the little parade eventually passed
and continued on towards the grey horizon, to the point where the long
line of the earth disappeared, and for several minutes I kept scratching
my head, trying to understand this mystery. But soon my irresistible old
friend, Dr. Indifference, lowered himself on to me, and I wandered off.

After Baudelaire's "Chacun sa chimère."

67. The Universal Ecstasy of Things

You're going to love this poem, believe me. It's a wonderful day
and this magnificent park is enraptured by the brilliant eye of the sun
like brilliant young people under the brilliant influence of love. I'm
talking about the universal ecstasy of things and how it's expressing
itself with each little peep. Even the fountains of the park are in a
kind of hypnotic state. We all know about riots in the street, but here
there is a riot of silence. I could just keep on writing forever. How,
for instance, an ever-increasing celestial radiance makes everything
sparkle and how the flowers are overcome with the maddening ambition
to rival the blue of the sky with the energy of their erotic colours,
and their horny fragrances rise into the warm air like hot smoke.

Nevertheless, my friend, amidst all this universal joy I noticed
a troubled man. He was a clown, a jester, a fool out of Shakespeare,
out of one of the plays Poe would have written had he lived, one of those
fools whose job it was to make kings smile when they were obsessed as
they often were with remorse, with boredom, with both, and he was all
decked out in a ridiculous costume with a hat of horns and handbells
and he was actually kneeling at the base of a pedestal on which stood
a colossal statue of Venus, and he was crying cats and dogs, and he
looked up at the face of the immortal goddess as if pleading with her.
"I am the most solitary, the most lost of all human beings," he said,
or he seemed to be saying, "I'm absolutely cut off from all forms of
love and friendship, I'm lower than the lowest. Yet even I have been
created with spiritual understanding and a sense of Absolute Beauty!
Oh, Goddess, have pity on my sadness, have pity on my loneliness, my
delirium." Need I go on? You know the rest. Venus didn't budge or sigh
but continued staring with a far-off look in her phony marble eye.

After Baudelaire's "Le Fou et la Vénus."

68. Jellyfish of Light

A huge jellyfish of light (only way to describe it) sprang up in the sky over
Petrozavodsk just before the last false dawn started telling the truth this morning,
it hovered over the city for ten minutes as it sent down a torrential rain of
light, a multitude of fine beams of light, before turning into a circular
aperture bright red in the centre, followed by more beams of torrential
light, even finer, and finally moved off in the direction of Finland. I
missed it of course, didn't open my blinds until noon that day. Besides,
I was in Moscow, dreaming you and I were slowly climbing opposite sides of
a pyramid with a dazzling eye at the top, a centre of light emitting fine
beams of light. We were half-blind and half-starved and it seemed as if we'd been
climbing for months, but we kept climbing and we knew some fine day we'd
meet at the top and our bodies would turn into light. I recalled an hour
spent with you a month or six ago and I recalled brilliant light and a kind
of unbelievably brilliant music never heard, never mind composed. Easy for
me to say, I'm just a poet, not a composer, it's not my job to become pure
spirit. Yes, they'll probably be talking about that light over Petrozavodsk
forever, but nobody talks about the brilliant jellyfish that bursts in my
mind when you phone to say you're free, unless I write about it, and even
then they might not, so I try hard to write well, and I become confused,
because when you try hard to write well all your passion becomes distant,
and you become afraid of losing your intimate contact with human
suffering by becoming pure spirit, by giving up on your suffering, which
may not be all that intense but it feels intense and it provides you with a
sympathetic and perhaps illusory understanding of the sufferings of saints,
not to mention quadriplegics, burn victims, the grief-stricken, the romantic.
No, I can't give it up, the starving don't want to hear poetic rhapsodies on
the metaphysics of light. It's easy to talk about light when you've just had
a plate of fish and chips, a jelly doughnut, and are sitting on the pier at
Key West watching the pink jellyfish bob in the waves as the sun sets.

And I bought a bottle of that perfume you like, it's yours the next time
you come, as long as you don't take forever! But I was sitting on the pier
and this dirty mutt came by, tongue hanging out, the kind of dog that
strikes you as being more intelligent than most people, and warier, the
kind of dog that looks as if he'd bite the throat of a baby in a crib if he
thought no one was looking. And so I said here doggy, come here doggy,
come here and take a whiff of my dear love's perfume bought at the best
store in the entire city. I figured you were never going to come again
anyway, it's so hopeless. And the dog, wagging its tail deliberately, like
a politician's smile, came up and put its wet nose against the open bottle,
then shrieked and snarled at me and backed away. And I thought, God, if I'd
offered this ugly mangy mutt a packet of human shit he'd have sniffed it
with delight and maybe even gobbled it up. You can't talk to dogs about
perfume, you can't talk to hungry people (and who isn't hungry?) about
the jellyfish of poetic light that bursts in my mind whenever we meet.

After Baudelaire's "Le Chien et le flacon." Baudelaire of course was unable to predict our new
generation of chemically sensitive people for whom perfume is a dangerous toxin.

69. Elephants on Television

I don't want to disillusion you, but it seems to me we swallow a lot of
things we shouldn't swallow and there comes a time we're forced to
cough them up, midnight agony with lightning bolts and the wailing
of demons giving birth to demons in the poisonous darkness out of which
light is born. Just when you think you've coughed up the final safety pin
or innertube or your mother's rhinestone sunglasses (circa 1952)
and are finally free you feel another foreign object working its way
loose at a lower level and looser and looser it gets until you find yourself
sitting up in bed all night waiting for it to come and it finally comes like
Jumbo's corpse. And you think hurray I'm free at last but there's more,
much more. What is it about life that makes us fear death? Surely not this
constant process of puking ourselves inside out? Give me oblivion any day.
But you call and say my star is shining higher in your heaven every night,
you've decided you want us to devote our lives (and fortunes) to each other,
or I sit here watching elephants on television, spending all day trying
to suck water with trunks buried in dry sand, or spending hours rubbing
bellies against a rock, trying to scrape out the deeply buried ticks, or
how they seem to be so moved when they come upon the rotted corpse of a
big bull and they go all over the bones with their sensitive trunks as if
trying to figure out how the old guy died, and then they carry the bones
singly off into the forest and bury them so other elephants I suppose
will be spared the grief of seeing such a sight. They want to live.
And so I am inspired to live, to try to rub the ticks out of my mind,
to continue the long process of purification, rather than giving up.

What we love in each other is our individuality and when one dies we
mourn the loss of that uniqueness that will never come again, and when
you love you pity those who died before the birth of the beloved for
they never had the opportunity to gaze upon such perfect loveliness,
even though you know they had beauty of their own to gaze upon and
that beauty is now long gone and inadequately recorded of course.
It seems so strange that we should have been born in this horrible
century. *We were not made for death and darkness.** The soul follows
the body around like a cloud and the cloud is just big enough to block
out the sun. I want you to stop reading right now and admit you're
really happy. Then let's get ahold of that fairy Lorca and take him out
to the garbage dump at the edge of town and fire a bullet into his head.

* Line from an old Dutch hymn sung at my cousin John Pidgeon's funeral.

70. Have a Nice Day

I've always told myself don't do anything unless it's absolutely necessary
or unless it'll bring in enough money to buy time to write more poetry.
But sometimes I'll shock myself by acting under some mysterious impulse
with a quickness and certainty of which I thought myself incapable.
I can keep a letter in my pocket for two weeks without daring to open it
or stare at my ringing phone for nine rings without daring to answer it.
And then suddenly without warning under some mysterious impulse like an
arrow from a bow find the most extraordinary courage to execute the most
absurd and bizarre and sometimes even dangerous action. For my soul is a
lazily sensuous one and finds it difficult to perform the simplest tasks—
but I'm a lot like my friend who set a forest on fire to see if the fire would
spread as quickly as the warnings indicated and who once lit a cigar beside
an open tank of gasoline on a whim. The ones who tend to manifest energy
like this, springing from boredom, are usually the laziest dreamers of all.

One morning I got up grumpy and bored with a long bout of idleness, threw
open my window and spotted this guy in the street selling large panes of
glass and hawking his wares with the loudest and ugliest cries imaginable.
I called out to him to come up, even though I knew he'd have a heckuva time
making his way up the narrow winding staircase to my room on the sixth floor,
especially while carrying his fragile and awkward merchandise. But the goof
finally made it and I examined his panes of glass, sighed and said, "What?
You don't have any coloured glass? No rose, no blue, no red, no panes of
transparent paradise? Have you no shame? How dare you come to this poor
part of town without bringing the kind of glass that would help to make
our lives appear more beautiful?" And I gave him a push towards the door.
I went out on the balcony, grabbed a little potted geranium, and when the
man finally came out on the street below I let the pot accidentally drop
straight down and it hit the ground and exploded right behind him. He was
so startled he fell over backwards on top of his sheets of glass with a
glittering crash that sounded like a crystal palace struck by lightning!
You can imagine how absolutely drunk with lunacy I felt! I was reeling!
But I was also a little shocked at my cruelty and felt some compassion
for the poor bugger who was only trying to make a living, probably had a
family at home, wondering if they were going to have meat for dinner.
So I put on a happy face and called down to him: "Have a nice day!"

After Baudelaire's "Le Mauvais Vitrier." The note of compassion in lines 32 to 34 is absent
in the original.

71. Star

You were smiling as you lay on the delivery table, and I held up the brilliant baby you'd just given birth to, so brilliant we had to close our eyes. We stared as the first brilliant point rose out of your birth canal and the second and third popped out together, then the fourth and fifth. A living five-pointed star brilliant as the sun, pulsing with solar power, and I held it up with a peculiar combination of exhilaration and sorrow. A geometrically perfect five-pointed star, so brilliant we felt we'd gone out of our minds, or inexplicably been shifted to a different universe. But we were brave, and you held out your weak arms and I gave it to you with a weak joke: This is what comes from being over-literal, a star is born. But this was no joke. This was something actually created from our conspiracy, something that had been growing inside you for nine months, and you held it and cradled it in your arms, tears running down your face, and you looked at me joyfully and said, Dave, what does this mean? And I had of course no answers. What will we call it? Let's call it Star. And it just sat warmly in your arms, in shining featureless geometric perfection, with no eyes but it was all one perfect eye, no mouth but all one perfect mouth, no mind but all one perfect mind, a small god more perfect than any god imaginable, a small star more perfect than anything in heaven, warm as any normal baby but not too warm, swimming in light and so peaceful we began to feel an outlandish, astonishing and incomprehensible tranquillity. As if we'd been chosen to give birth to something that had some kind of divine destiny. Something perfect, radiant, original and destined for terrible fame.

Something simple. Something no one else had. Something undoubtedly destined to be more famous than the Dionne Quints. Just wait till the reporters hear about this, I muttered, and you continued quietly sobbing and smiling, each tear with a perfect tiny five-pointed star reflected.

From the Portuguese.

72. Conversation with a Small Herd of Cattle

I didn't want to go to the camera store with Walter, I wanted to stay home
and finish reading *Crime and Punishment*. It was a fantabulous spring day
in Cranbrook, I only had a chapter to go, but I didn't read a word while he
was gone. Just sat there staring dully at the wall, and at one point I thought
the roof was leaking but it was only Ink Spot, Walter's cat, noisily sucking
his paws. I got into a staring contest with the cat and it looked as if there'd
never be a winner as the light in the room began to dim and sweet afternoon
dissolved into mournful evening. But Walter's car pulled up and Ink Spot
turned his head to the window. I didn't read a word, I told Walter, I had a
two-hour staring contest with Ink Spot. Walter wanted to know who won.

The next morning I was strolling down a country lane just outside town
and as I strolled I was reading a book by C. S. Lewis. Apple and cherry
blossoms were everywhere and Lewis was talking about Egyptian
priests at the time of and according to Herodotus being able to trace
their ancestry back 145 generations. Maybe it was just the mood
but the small herd of cattle at the side of the road appeared almost
human. Maybe it was the charm of this isolated valley in the spring,
maybe it was the charm of Lewis, Herodotus and the blossoms combined
but the herd seemed just like us, and they called me over for a chat.
They seemed unduly sensitive at first, but maybe I was simply
annoying them with my questions. "They'll never kill me," said
one young bull when I asked if he resented knowing his days were
numbered. I asked one lovely young cow if she resented being owned,
a mere piece of property, and she said absolutely not, life is lovely
here in the valley, lots of contentment, blossoms, thick rich clover.
I told them how surprised I was to be standing there chatting with
cattle as if they were human. "Well," said the bull, "we are just like
humans in many ways but few humans realize it." I asked if he could
explain why I never noticed this all my life till now. "Our sympathetic
perceptions often improve with age," he said, and he began telling me
that some members of the *Bovidae* family had actually mated with
humans, in fact there had been genetic accidents from time to time
resulting in crossbreeds, things you never read about in the papers,
and he gave me the name of one rather prominent family descended
from such a crossbreed and my mouth gaped with shock for the
family he mentioned was one to which I was distantly related. I
was part cow, no wonder I could communicate with them. And when
the next day I finished typing this poem down to this line I sat back
and closed my eyes for a moment. When I opened them a hummingbird
was hovering in front of me. I blinked. It drifted out the window.

73. Hell

After writing two minimalist love poems I later tore to pieces and threw
away because they were so disgusting (they really were!) I went to visit
some friends and they were talking about some woman they'd heard had
jumped from the twenty-fourth floor and there was a guy watching TV
and drinking beer on the first floor and when he heard the thud as she
hit the ground he ran out and dragged her warm body behind the trees
and raped her. And then they got talking about the girl who murdered
the cabbie and cut off his genitals and glued them to her body with
Crazy Glue. I went a little crazy myself, called my friends a pair of
ghouls, stomped out, but later noticed the story in my typewriter was
about a young fellow who'd been studying for the priesthood, had some
serious problems with his mother, ended up killing her, then cutting off
his penis and stuffing it down her throat, sewed her mouth shut over it,
cut off her head and tried to set it on fire. He had blonde hair, blue eyes
and a voice like an angel's. I'd gone to my friends because I was having
trouble describing the look in his eyes, how to describe it, as he paced
his cell, for he looked at me as if he understood totally what he had done
and he wanted me or anyone else who happened by simply to know he
understood more than anyone what he had done, for his eyes were tender
and wild and pleading with me to forgive him or at least to give him a
little look that would indicate I felt there was some possibility of him
someday becoming human again (although it seemed doubtful that they'd
ever let him be a priest now), and at the same time his eyes said he knew
that no one anywhere in all the corridors of time could ever forgive him.
Even the guy in the next cell, who had killed twenty children by offering
them money to help him look for his puppy then taking them into the woods
and hammering four-inch spikes into their heads, couldn't forgive him.

Artaud, who said of himself that his thoughts were like razorblades, that
his heart and mind despised each other with total justification, that he
was being burned at the stake of his own brilliance, that what was true
of him was true for everyone, and that things were even worse than even
he could say, might have forgiven him. And last week a young fellow, the
same age as the fair-haired angel, asked me how to go about getting your
poems published, and the angel's tender eyes began flickering in my mind
and I told him about the importance of a stamped, self-addressed envelope.

74. Green

Baudelaire said he had to write about hell, all the other subjects
were in use and he didn't want to be unoriginal or take the chance of
annoying a possessive poet. He died in his mother's arms, like Christ.
The painter Mondrian hated the colour green so much he would often
head out to the suburbs of Paris in the middle of the night with a
shovel strapped to his bicycle and dig up lawns. You are sitting across
from me as I write and you are wearing your wine sweater and a green
silk scarf. I decided to write about what was in front of me and when I
looked up there you were. You are smiling, I am happy to see you in the
flesh rather than simply hearing your disembodied voice on the phone.
You make everyone else seem so boring! You start telling me stories about
Miles Davis, how he was depressed one night, a friend suggested they
get an orgy organized and Miles said nah, I don't wanna put these
million-dollar lips on no two-dollar pussy. How he was racing to a gig
one night and smashed into a tree with his Ferrari and when they were
prying him loose from the wreckage, both legs broken, he said he
didn't wanna go to that gig anyway. I showed you a photo of a park,
a Rick/Simon photo taken from an unusual angle half-way between
standing up and bending over daintily for a drink from the fountain.
Ordinarily in this position one wouldn't stop to observe the park but would
merely continue bending or standing up straight. One wouldn't notice
the fire hydrant like a little poet stuck in the lawn off to one side and one
would not notice the painter Mondrian, standing outside the right frame,
scowling, wishing he could paint the whole park orange. The benches
are just sitting there exactly where they were placed and it's as if they
are trying to pretend they don't care if anyone ever sits on them. There
used to be a magnificent series of renaissance fountains in this park but
they were removed because they proved too costly for the city to maintain.
They are stored in the city hall basement, waiting for another renaissance.

The strong must be gentler than the weak and the ego resembles the snout
of a pig or the nozzle of an industrial-strength vacuum cleaner. We must
believe for every drop of rain that falls something like four or five just
can't be bothered falling. The Kamikaze pilots of Japan gave their lives
so that the women and children of Japan would not perish under American
bombardment. In the suburbs people are playing tennis and the trees are
about to turn green again. A grade 12 student is sitting on his front step
watching two robins fighting over an earthworm and he says: "I know I'm
going to be late for my biology class but this is more interesting." Poetry
contains Vitamin P. You can die from lack of what is to be found in poetry.
For instance, the students feel as if they are in jail for it's the first day of
spring so we read translations of Ho Chi Minh's prison poems and the
kids start feeling better, some of them even start writing little poems
almost as good as Ho's. On this lovely spring day I keep thinking about
the Kamikaze pilots of Japan and wondering if I could ever be that
courageous. Later, on the subway, an old man is singing a song from his
youth. He is self-conscious but determined. When I look the poor old guy
stops singing and when I turn away he shyly starts again, so I don't look.

75. Membrane of Bliss

One of these mornings somebody's going to wake up with a sense of having
lost his sense of loss, as if graduated finally from the carefully graduated
daily dull swamp of pain. What lies under the world is the core of it, it has
always been dull fear, dim and flagrant longings, the demons that thrive
on buckets of hard booze and sorrow. One of these mornings somebody's
going to look at his sorrow directly and see the intelligent light that has
always been there and always will, so that he feels for a moment as if he's
a cube of sugar dissolving in a pail of pale honey, and the fleeting moment
is Moby Dick in disguise. Now we have graduated we can do with all our power
all our duty. We've become free to avoid self-destruction and to practise
self-possession and the divinity of our animated cartoons. The occasional
streetsweeper or garbage truck roars by on the street outside my apartment
which might as well be vacant because for several hours I'll be invisibly
bathing in darkness. I lock up, barricade myself into my deliriously serene
and cosmic solitude, a membrane of bliss that isolates me from urban life.

Let's see now. Today I met with several men of letters, one of whom asked me
if one could travel to New Mexico by way of land (he must have thought
New Mexico might be in the South Seas), and I quarrelled (generously) with
an editor who responded to each of my complaints by saying, "But we're all
honest here." I said hello to about twenty people, of whom fifteen were
total strangers. I distributed handshakes in the same proportion. Remember
to buy a pair of gloves! It rained, and I sought shelter by visiting a certain
notorious lady who asked me to design her some kind of New Wave outfit
in purple leather! I dropped in to see a theatrical director who suggested I
collaborate on a writing project with that sensational new playwright whose
name is on everyone's lips and whom he described as being the dullest,
stupidest and most celebrated of all his authors. I boasted inexplicably
about some villainous act I never actually committed, and denied in the
most cowardly fashion another villainous act I actually did commit—and
with glee! Refused to lend a hand to a very good friend of mine who needed
help, yet gave a warm and positive letter of recommendation to this guy
I've always despised. And so I am annoyed with myself, as always, and
annoyed with everyone I know. And in nocturnal solitude I really want
to make amends and perhaps try to retrieve a measure of self-respect. In
the silence and darkness, reviewing my crimes and offences of the day,
I pray to the souls of those I love, the souls of those I write about, to beg
for strength and sustenance. I want to remove myself from the stench and
falseness of the world, and I pray to God to accord me the grace to produce
a few more beautiful poems which would prove at least to myself that I am
not the very least of men, and that I am not inferior to those I most despise.

After Baudelaire's "Une Heure du Matin." Baudelaire, obsessed with trying to purify himself
spiritually, for a while practised the Kabbalistic ritual of reviewing the events of the day before
falling asleep at night.

76. My Chocolate Maserati

These things happen. Rostropovich has become more interesting than the
Rolling Stones. I can't read without glasses. My joints creak. I exasperate
all my old friends with my lack of enthusiasm for anything but Plotinus
and questions of ethical values. My dearest and oldest friends can't take me
for more than five minutes, and so I try to pursue dignity through solitude,
with no interest in risking boredom never mind asphyxiation for warmth.
My heart, full moon that never wanes, provides such warmth as I need.
I get up in the morning, stare at the wall all day, and go to bed at night.
The joy of this pleasure far surpasses the agonies of love and friendship.
A good poet if he lives always reaches his peak past the age of seventy
and so I'm getting ready, have even started dozing off unshaven in the
public library. Better than dozing off naked in a parked car with the
motor running. A poet in Victoria writes complaining about her latest
tragic love affair and I reply (hypocritically) that nothing is better for
poetry than boredom, breakups, breakdowns. And maybe breakfasts.
Better to say poetry thrives on quietness and growing old. You can't
write anything worthwhile until you notice that Death has noticed you.

She writes she had a dream in which I inherited a million dollars and was
driving around in a chocolate-coloured Maserati. I tell her it's true but
the money is all in a trust fund for my many children, and the problem
with the Maserati is its colour: the kids think it's real chocolate and tend
to slobber all over it. I tell her I'll never forget a moment of the year of
"absolute insanity" and "incredible joy" we shared, but in truth by golly I've
forgotten nine-tenths of it, like dumping soggy excess baggage. I reminded
her, speaking of chocolate, how we used to get up at noon and head down
to the village for boxes of chocolate bars for breakfast and that if we'd
seen a chocolate Maserati in those days we'd have tried to eat it. After I
mailed the letter I remembered that she (and I) never ate chocolate.

77. Walter's Moustache

When she met Walter for the first time she touched his moustache lovingly and said, "Oh no, you haven't grown a moustache!" No, Grandma, I said, that's Walter, I'm over here. Her mind had sparked back, it appeared, to her first husband who'd been dead sixty years. In his photos he had a moustache just like Walter's. She'd been married fifty years to her second husband, but her mind had its secret flashbacks to her first. And her second entered the room as if he'd been reading minds again, and began speaking of her first husband, what a good man he was although they'd never met, how he was a pacifist, and never would have fired his rifle at another man, he told people before he left for France in 1917 that under no circumstances would he ever shoot at another human being, he could speak seven languages, he only went off to war because he didn't want to humiliate his parents by having everyone in that little Yorkshire town think he was a coward, and he was shot down in the first minute of his first battle and was killed. Tears were streaming down the old man's face, and it occurred to me he'd be dead soon and when he died husband one would be in heaven waiting.

Smiling, with a reassuring handshake. You have no idea the dreams you have when you're in your eighties, said my grandmother. People who've been dead for sixty years appear and you can see them so clearly you can almost reach out and touch them. And she reached out again to touch Walter's moustache. Her dim eye said she was thinking of husband one again and I wondered if husband two realized it and if it made him sad at all. No, by the time you've reached that age you've absorbed in your life so much sadness a little more sadness wouldn't affect you at all. They've witnessed the century to end all centuries, and yet still the seasons change, sadness accumulates and makes us wise, and we die to make room for the young, who are really the same as us all over again but in a different disguise.

78. Another Plate of Fudge

He was well-groomed and well-dressed and he stopped me on the street
and asked for a quarter. Usually when I give these guys a quarter they're
not satisfied, they say give me another one willya, I need it for the subway,
I've lost my family, and if you give them a second quarter they decide
they need a steak dinner, or a place to spend the night. So my policy is to
give a quarter and when they ask for more say that's all I can afford, I'm
only a poet, and furthermore I live in the neighbourhood, I get hit six times
a block. And when I tell them that their voices soften and they ask if they can
lend me money, they tell me they get money from an average of one out of
every hundred people they ask, the rest pretend they don't hear or see them.
This one old smelly rotten guy asked for a quarter and when I gave him one
he told me I'd for sure go to heaven when I died, and he said, "By the way, I
can draw power from the ground up through my legs and make my heart
shine like a searchlight." I knew somewhere Plato mentioned someone
who could draw raw power from the ground like that, and it reminded me
that sometimes life is like reading, though usually when you read you
take things out of the common pool and put them in the little tub of your
life, and when you write the opposite process takes place. For instance,
it's well known that if a poet writes poetry on a plane he won't get jet lag,
or if he writes poetry before playing tennis he's more likely to win, or if
he burns himself just after writing a poem the burn won't give pain and
will heal without blistering or leaving a mark, or if he gets drunk after
writing poetry he won't get a hangover. And once I dreamt that in the core
of my brain was a giant eye, closed tightly, sound asleep, snoring in fact.

The dream came years ago, when I was reading Plato even though I had no need
(at the time) for philosophical consolation (or so I thought). What was that
eye? Was it a Freudian dream pun? Is it still in the same place, and still
tightly shut after all those years? The truth is it opens and closes. If it
would only stay open all the time all my problems would be problems. The
fool persisting in his folly becomes wise, the magician persisting in his
magic finds his inner eye opening all the time, the eye that once open sees
so clearly the formlessness of everything and refuses to abide by the basic
patterns the ego imposes on the cosmos. But talking about the opening of the
inner eye has a tendency to cause it to close itself. And if that's the case
then maybe it should bloody well be closed. I either am or want to be
completely disinterested. Everyone needs a mountain to fall off. And as I
write the moon stops flickering, the roses in the garden stop flickering,
and on the surface of the lake the ripples disappear, except for the ripples
caused by the occasional falling leaf. In the pub the poetry circle has
ordered another round of cremes de cacao and another plate of fudge, and
somewhere someone feels an inexpressible sadness because his sadness is
inexpressible. Because power does not come up from the ground, demons do.
David and the ambiguities. Energy is eternal delight, the stuff dreams are
made of, but we do not wish to partake of this eternal delight because we
fear, perhaps, abandoning our own humanity, and somewhere in our hearts
we know we'll bloody well partake of it for all eternity once we're dead.

79. My Brother's Poetry

Glenn Gould dropped in and started playing Bach's Two and Three Part
Inventions on the little Yamaha which by chance I'd just had tuned.
And my father wouldn't listen, he kept telling me stories about being
on a ship in the Arctic Ocean during the war. He was telling me how
certain things came to be and he told me all about the war and how it
started. I kept confusing oceans and deserts. He said the ocean is like the
lake only bigger and the desert is like the beach only bigger. Then I was
on my father's ship, standing at his side, Bach still in the air, as the ship
passed through a narrow channel between two mountains of ice. It was
scary as being born. I told my father how brave he was. "I'm not brave,
son," he said, gravely, "in fact I'm seriously considering killing myself,
and by God I am going to kill myself." With that he jumped off the ship
and landed on top of one of the mountains of ice. "Wait for me, dad," I
shouted, and soon I was on top of the mountain with him. It wasn't all that
cold. We slid down the other side like a pair of penguins. At the bottom
there were some little houses. It looked like Hiroshima on the final morning.
Babies were being born, men and women making love, parachutes appeared
to be falling slowly. Picasso came up to me, did a happy little dance,
and slapped me on the back. William Blake went into the outhouse and
slammed the door. I remembered I'd been arguing with Glenn Gould about
who was the greater artist, Blake or Picasso, he chose Blake and I Picasso.

I wandered through the narrow streets and found the farmhouse where my
Uncle Cecil and Aunt Clara used to live. This was the hill I tried to climb
when I was a kid. It wasn't a mountain of ice then. It wasn't dangerous.
It was sunny and there was a bluebird on every fencepost. You could hear
a cow moo three miles away. All this really happened long ago, and it
somehow explains everything: now I know why I am the way I am and why
you are the way you are. You are with me. We're all climbing down ladders.
My brother is acting smart. He too threatens to kill himself, then falls
accidentally off his ladder and down the mountain of ice. He falls slowly
like a parachute bomb. You try to save him by pulling on the rope
but as you pull it his head falls off. You become almost hysterical. My
father appears and puts his coat over my brother's body. He picks up the
head and puts it under the blanket too. He is serene. "I was expecting
something like this," he says, oddly untroubled. "He'd been acting so
strangely lately. He wasn't always like this." My father pulls out an old
book of poems authored by my brother. They are beautiful poems, with
long exquisite lines that branch out and seem to reach up to heaven. No
poems like them. Nice edition too. I had no idea my brother could write such
poetry and suddenly I'm crying. And there's a blinding explosion of light.

80. The Taming of the Shark

You were sleeping on the sunny sand at Pompano Beach a hundred feet
from the surf, the shark came walking out of the water on its fins,
attacked you as you slept, you recovered, joked about the incident,
called it a confrontation between athlete and intellect much to the
delight of the paramedics and there was the time you lifted the cover
of a manhole for lack of anything better to do and saw the same shark
swimming in the cold clear stream of the kind of sewer you see in dream
and you could see right to the bottom so clear was the stream. On the
bottom shining clearly was a large pile of gold coins, you dived in for
the gold without a thought and emerged badly bruised but rich. Now you
say there are caves in the ocean floor where sharks congregate to spend
hours narcotized by the oxygen-rich fresh-water springs which make them
gentler than lambs, gentler than llamas, even gentler than lamas, so
gentle you can swim among them without fear, the springs also have a
beneficial effect on their sweet thick hides, kill all their parasites.

So now you tell me that you have captured that shark, have tamed it,
and it has become as lovable as tiger lilies. It swims quietly in its
own small tank, a tight fit. And it has no mate. Not a good situation
for a shark to be in. What if it reverts to its original ferocity?
Get it a larger tank, a mate, I say, but you ignore me. I am its keeper,
you persist in an unearthly monotone, I have to monitor its oxygen
intake, I have to make sure it has a balanced diet, I have to be continually
reassuring it, telling it I love it and so on, like a horse. I have to give it
exercises to do, little weights to lift, I have to make it feel appreciated.
I have to spend hours standing there staring at it through the glass.

After a poem by Susan Musgrave.

81. Consciousness

You wander through each chartered street stopping people and asking them what consciousness is. "Golly, I don't know," they say. But someone, when you ask him, says, "All I know is everything that was living turned to rock when consciousness appeared." So I ask you what consciousness is and you say it's a huge rock floating in the air. You ask if I'm interested in coincidence and when I say yes I surely am you say what a coincidence so am I. Snow has fallen all through the night and now it is lying around in drifts six feet high. Together we get down on our knees and pray that when the snow has all melted we'll still be here, reading novels by Frederick Philip Grove. You pick up one, and read aloud to me: "This country seems to have been created to rouse man's consciousness to the fullest extent." I ask if you've read *Anne of Green Consciousness*. You say you've seen the play. Consciousness, you say, is a picky eater. It's a cow with no udder. A snake with no tail, at least none worth telling. Consciousness fits like a glove, it fills the room and seeps out through the smallest crack. Later, in the Metro Library, we're facing each other across the table and I'm reading the *Oxford Companion to Consciousness*. Suddenly I open my mouth and breathe the word "consciousness." You seem annoyed, you sigh and shift your legs. You are trying to read your book, *A Hundred Years of Consciousness*. You leap to the table and shout as loud as you can, "I always try to enjoy myself as much as possible without disturbing others." Everyone ignores you. The snow keeps falling, and I pray it will continue falling and we'll have to spend the night together in the library. How romantic! You slip me a note. It reads: Consciousness is right around the corner. I say let's go right now.

So the snow has stopped and at two in the morning we are strolling past Carlo's Pizzeria and although it's closed there's a private party going on and we barge in, holding hands, speaking in unison: "Hi fellas, sure hope you don't mind us barging in like this. We were just strolling by and saw people in here. It looked like a private party, but we didn't think you'd mind if we came in and said hello. Basically we just wanted to know what you were talking about, it looked so interesting from the street." They look alarmed. "Don't be alarmed," you say. "He's a somnambulist and I'm a researcher with a special interest in the field of consciousness. So please just ignore us. Pretend we're not here. We promise not to disturb you."

82. Perceptual Error

He looks like a man who somewhere along the line has made a fundamental
error in his life, like everyman in other words, but unlike most men he is
lying naked in a snowbank at Spadina and Bloor reciting lines from Allen
Ginsberg's *Howl* in a calm voice. A pair of cops pick him up and throw him
in the cruiser. A stern-looking woman approaches me, I know she's going
to ask for a dollar for a hamburger so before she does I reach in my pocket,
get out a handful of change, and hand it to her. She's surprised but she
won't let on, and the change falls through her hand and lands on the sidewalk.
I bend down and pick it all up and put it in her hand carefully this time.
Suddenly I'm driving north through Southern Alberta and there's a thunderstorm
in the sky to my right, another thunderstorm in the sky to my left, but the
sky in front of me is clear and full of stars. It is midnight and the lights
of a small foothill town twenty miles away can be seen on the horizon and one
of the lights keeps getting brighter then dimmer then abruptly as my car
climbs a rise in the road the light flies up into the sky and I realize it
isn't a light from the town at all but the tip of the crescent moon, and for
miles as I drive that hilly road through Southern Alberta the moon dips up
and down, slides up and down, appearing and disappearing behind the horizon.

Halfway through the second part of a Greta Garbo double bill the audience
starts hollering at me to leave, they can't hear the soundtrack because I
can't stop coughing. I stumble out to the lobby to get some cider and the
snackbar is closed but there's a little sign saying help yourself and a plate
in which to leave the money. I get a cup and open the cider tap but it breaks
off in my hand. So I run across the street and get some coughdrops then go
back in to sit without coughing and continue contemplating Greta's wonderful
nose, wondering if she's still alive and if so where is she and would she
like it if I wrote and asked her to tell me the story of her life so I could
write it up in a book. At movie's end I take the broken tap to the manager with
the intention of apologizing for breaking it and offering to try to help him
fix it or failing that I'd be glad to pay for it but before I get a chance he
starts yelling at me in front of the people who were earlier yelling at me.
Why did you try to get cider when no one was here? he yells, mad as a grade 5
teacher. I throw the tap at him and stomp out. I stick my nose in the hall
next door and a priest from Ottawa in an expensive suit is addressing a
meeting of the Jungian Society and is telling them individuation is the work
of a lifetime. On the subway a sensitive-looking man in a cowboy hat sits
quietly looking straight ahead while a drunk with no hat at all looks at him
and says you're not a cowboy, you're not smart enough. In the Costa Rican
rainforest a bright red bird catches a butterfly in its beak and shakes
off its shiny slightly iridescent blue wings before eating it. Practise love
on animals, says Gurdjieff. They are more sensitive and respond better.

83. Crime Prevention Measures

The government is proposing a number of measures designed to prevent
the commission of crimes. Not tonight dear I have to re-pot the violets.
"My God!" he exploded. "Where have you been gone, woman? You've been
gone hours, hours, and in a storm like this! What the hell do you go to that
bloody wood for? What have you been up to? It's hours even since the
rain stopped, hours! Do you know what time it is? You're enough to drive
anybody mad. Where have you been? What in the name of hell have you
been doing?" Persons convicted of second-degree murder will not be
eligible for parole until they've completed ten years of their sentences.
Not tonight dear we're out of camembert. "Don't! Don't go! Don't leave me!
Don't be cross with me! Hold me fast!" she whispered in blind frenzy, not
even knowing what she said, and clinging to him with uncanny force.
Persons convicted of either first or second-degree murder will not be
permitted unescorted temporary absences or day paroles by the Parole Board
until they have completed all but three years of the non-parolable portion
of their sentences. Certain weapons are already prohibited. Not tonight
dear I can't find my glasses. He spread out his hand with a gesture, and
then he sneezed, sneezing away the flowers from his nose and his navel.
The implementation of all these measures will take time. Not tonight dear
the budgies are moulting. Mother, here is Thy virtue, here is Thy vice.
Take them both and grant me only pure love for thee. If released on parole,
an offender will remain on parole for the rest of his life. Not tonight dear
my mother's got a headache. Besides my imagination's not up to it. He
portrayed Mrs. Dick as an adult possessed of rich imaginative powers, who
lived in a strange world of fantasy. As a child she had created for herself
a beautiful dream world, and sometimes these children never grow up, their
dream world never disappears. Not tonight dear life is too short. Not tonight
dear your hair's on fire. Not tonight dear I'm creating a beautiful dream world.

Making love to you is like being swallowed by a giant anaconda. A sound
love dwells only in a sound person (Kawabata). Not tonight dear I've just
taken a shower/found out I've got lung cancer/got a piece of food stuck
in my tooth. When glances that have been wandering at the same level of
consciousness meet, each seems to probe the other to its depths (Yokomitsu).

With lines from *Lady Chatterley's Lover* and *The Gospel of Sri Ramakrishna*.

84. Sailing in Perfect Space

You know we're travelling to the same place, you know we will meet there,
you know we can't travel together, I know you know all this and that it's
raining and I left my umbrella at home, I know I'll walk home through
the rain, you will be so far ahead of me I won't be able to see you, and
by the time I get home I'll have no idea where you are, but I will sit
down at the piano and imagine you standing there with your eyes burning
and your violin under your chin, ready to start playing. I'm amused,
relaxed, and at this moment a man I've never met is sitting alone in the
room where I was born and he has a knife in his hand and is working up
the courage to use it on himself. In my dreams people I've never met but
about whom you've spoken, your mother and father for instance, tell me
what a wonderful person you are and how happy they are that you have
finally met me. They tell me that you stand to inherit a million dollars.
I know, I say, even though I don't know how I know, you never told me.
Even if you don't, I know we'll never tire (oh what horrible sentimentality)
of each other's foolishness. Why are we locked together like this (how can I
be writing this boozy slop?), by interlocking bands of light? Because as soon
as we take our foolishness seriously, which we certainly do (what's this gonna
sound like a year from now?), we discover our souls, they open up inside us
like magic books opening to exactly the right page when you glance at them.
And from then on everything changes. At least we'll never be the same again.
I was going to say that fame was a particularly notorious perversion of love
but then when you think about it, what isn't? Who am I to talk, sitting here
thoughtfully writing poetry when I'd rather be paddling down the Saugeen
on a still July afternoon, with real cows and real green fields and real woods.
My God, this simply isn't true. If I wanted to be paddling I would be paddling.
I don't know why I write all these lies. Why can't I be more like Edgar Guest?
Everything you want is yours as soon as you want it, if you really want it, that
is, not just if you think it's smart to say you want it or even to make yourself
think you want it when you have no need of it at all, or even if you simply
need it and don't know you want it. Our affections are like rabbits and soon
the world will be overrun with them. I will become any man you want
before you know you want him. When we're together, you know this but
I want you to see it on the page, we become spirits and nobody can see us.
Objectify everything has always been my motto, and believe me I'm trying.

Human thought is an expression of God's hate for His universe. Drinking
can take you straight to hell, as prayer can take you straight to heaven.
Lowry was horrified by the fame his book brought him, he said fame was
a treacherous kiss that exposed "that you have worked only for this."
A cloud goes by and it looks like a sow with a litter of piglets. I'm alone
on the beach on a misty October morning and it starts to rain frogs and
snakes and every so often a pineapple or a watermelon float down in a little
parachute. And bushel baskets full of grapes. This planet is dead, according
to the neoplatonists, because humanity has soaked up and isolated all its living
spirit. All the uninhabited planets, the planets that have wisely refused to evolve
intelligent life, are alive, like perfect Buddhas sailing in perfect space.

85. Early Autumn Guitar

Another wasted night, the full moon blurred through thin wet clouds,
and I trying both to forget you and not to forget you at the same time
although little in these poems is what it seems to be, I've graduated
from irony to ambiguity in the length of time it takes to do so (longer
than it takes to string a guitar, not as long as it takes to learn to play).
My attempts to extricate you from my heart seem cowardly, my desire to
keep my memories of you fresh and constant foolishly courageous. This
is not what I thought life would be like, but the moon though dimmed
has never seemed so close, whispering to me of serenity, faithfulness
and endless renewal. Perhaps this has nothing to do with you, this is
my attempt to use a dilemma of my own creation to breathe fresh music
into my mind as you revivify yourself with your secret late-night calls.
They say the soul secretly seeks out sadness to bring itself to life, to
remind its creatures of its own unwavering divinity, and if this is so I
must be on the verge of a great awakening. Only the creatures are judged
to be different, not the soul that animates them from within, and perhaps
only through this awakening will we be able to find ourselves together
once again, invisibly but indivisibly. Gypsy guitars accompany me
on my nightly solitary strolls through the early autumn avenues, I am
alone one moment and flooded with your invisible presence the next,
quietly, the quietness I felt in you, strongly, the strength I felt in you,
helplessly, the helplessness I loved in you, beautifully, the crazy beauty
you brought me and its sanity. Yet these rapturous nights appear and are lost,
the world loses all its value, becomes a cosmic garbage dump, the world
has nothing to offer true lovers but the great emancipation of death, the death
that comes whenever you think of it, the long-trapped energy of life
suddenly and ecstatically free. My friends wonder at my lack of desire,
and since I don't wish to alarm them I start new projects until I'm
back on track with people to meet, articles to write, classes to teach,
contracts to sign, and I go on crazy little spending sprees, a new
wardrobe, expensive electronic gadgetry, and I take all this new stuff
home and unwrap it and say hello darling to each new thing I unwrap.
And everything's all right except I'm doing all these things without a
sense of expectation, nothing is going to come from all of this, the world
has nothing to offer, but I am burning again and suddenly I see there are
certain tasks only I can perform, certain modest problems only I can solve.

Words are tropical fish that disport and distort themselves beneath the surface.
And so I swim in a pool of thick warm words and at night dream of wondrous
pigmented sentences lying in tubes waiting to be uncapped and squeezed.
Every word I write will have to be cancelled and I hope it can be by me.
Yet there is a Great Word from which all words come and that word is the
unspeakable word that means you-at-rest-in-my-soul-and-I-in-yours.

86. Listen to the Angels

The angels are speaking to you. Listen to them, no matter how unblakean
they may seem to be. The angels who speak to you are always the angels
you need, and you need to be told that you have embarked on the great
silence. Think of it as an adventure. Think of yourself as forming a small
joyful silence in a noisy world, a small pool of quiet and unregarded light
in a world of darkness. You say you've become sad and stupid, your friends
have forsaken and forgotten you. You alternate between blaming them
and blaming yourself, but there is no blame. Since you would not turn
against the world the world had to turn against you. The world races
towards you and at the last moment turns away like a Count Dracula
confronting a small pool of quiet and unregarded light. You have
done all this yourself, unknowingly, and the angels have been watching.
You ask what you should do, for yourself, for others, but there is nothing
for you to do. For now, and perhaps for the rest of your life, anything
you turn your hand to will end disastrously. And, because you know this,
you're not sad and stupid, but truly blessed, truly fortunate. If you
realize fully the danger you are in, there is no evil you need fear. So be
joyous, remain immersed in your little pool of quiet light. The angels
are not impressed by your tears, in fact no one is, least of all you.
You know your tears are the product of self-deceit. You have loved well,
and you have not been rewarded with the objects of your love. But if you
think this is a tragedy worthy of anything but the mildest touch of sorrow
then you're indeed a fool. There's no need to be strong, or weak, just quiet.

Oh, the danger you are in. Listen to the angels, they will keep you safe.
You say your grief has made you puerile, but if you hadn't been so puerile
you would never have felt such grief. Listen to the angels, listen to their
innocent chatter, for they have been attracted by the ridiculous power
of your love. For years they have been calling you to awaken to their light.
And now, finally, life has you checkmated, blocked off in all directions,
enchained, imprisoned. And this is what you have wanted all along, this
is what you have lived for, strived for. And now you have it. Be silent.

87. Baby Birds

Their beaks are open wide, their blind eyes and pitiful little cries
render the mother paradoxically incapable of action. She is gazing
helplessly into the nest. She's fat and healthy. Quickly becoming bored.
Her babies want something she cannot give. A certain kind of *wormth*
currently unavailable. She knows they will not starve to death, she
knows they will eventually accept her offerings. This is a picture
of your current dilemma. It is time to tell your babies to open their
eyes and shut their beaks. To maintain a dignified silence. To be still
and silent, scarcely breathing. No one is going to die today. Mother
and babies will soon be flying south together. It's only natural.
Even birds can become checkmated, paralyzed by chance events.

You must remember the strength in your soul's depths. The oracle
speaks of a stability that is stronger than fate. You must forget the
strength of your adversaries, for they know not what they do, or
if they do they know not why they do it. This is a period of oppression,
you do not know how such oppression came to be, but there is no need
to blame yourself, to drink to excess, to slash your wrists. All your
sins are forgiven. Consider that the angels might merely be playing
games with you, they are testing your character, they want to know
if you have the strength for the coming years. So go ahead, prove
you do. It would be untactful of me to tell you to be of good cheer,
when you find yourself in such a dilemma, but you have to realize
this dilemma is your dilemma, an unexpected development in your
line of fate, but one amazing in its implications. It's obviously time
for you to open your heart to the galaxies, to all of eternity, and when
you emerge from these dark times that seem now to stretch out in all
directions, if you ever do, nothing will have changed. You will be
as strong (or weak) as you always were and as blessed (or damned).

88. The Piano Player

Thanks for the card: the piano, the breeze-puffed curtain, the sheet
music lying on the floor. Your apology was appreciated, but I can't
recall what you did that was so terrible. I don't want to suggest I know
more about your secret heart than you do yourself, madame, but perhaps
you're really apologizing for some far greater sin, the unforgiveable
(almost) sin of not being with me all the time. An older man, small,
skinny, came to my office one day a while ago when I had just had four
wisdom teeth removed. I told him the pain was so severe I couldn't
concentrate on what he was saying. He said if I let him hypnotize me
the pain would go away. I said okay, anything to shut you up. And so
he hypnotized me, and although the pain did not abate even slightly,
it didn't bother me any more. It became an endearing sort of pain, a
little friend, a pathetic little old alarm clock ringing amorously in
the other room, not the one where the piano's playing. And that's
the way I feel now all the time. The spirit is everywhere, patiently
even joyfully waiting for the world to discover it. And all is well.

It's a game of hide-and-seek. It's so pleasant lying here behind the
moonlit bush, waiting for your friends to discover you, you hope they
never will discover you, and you will be waiting here forever. With
every breath the intensity of your shameless solitude increases, and with
glassy-eyed curiosity you wonder just how intense it will eventually
become. There's no end to it. You write poetry, it's wonderful! You
put it out into the world and the world is not bowled over. So what?
Loneliness and failure are the parents of all rhyme. Bunny Lang made a
black dunce-cap decorated with silver bells for Frank O'Hara to wear
when he wrote. She said it would keep him relaxed, and drive away the
spooks. She was glamorous and aloof. She telephoned him every morning
at eleven, and they would discuss, for an hour or two, everything they'd
thought of or dreamt since the previous day's call. Someone last week
asked me what I did for stimulation. I said I had no program, it's best
to be passive, and trust that exactly what you need will always come.

89. That Great Diamond Ring in the Sky

Can the argument with the self enter a new phase and pick up steam
at the same time? You have to be strong to pick up steam. Some people write
for newspapers, some people write poetry. But your old poems are eyes
staring at you from other and darker positions along time's huge diamond
ring in the sky. They were written for you though you pretend they were
written for others so the others will leave you alone and let you write.

The more humour you have the more you get humoured. Is this poetry we're
speaking of or something you call poetry in order to be left alone? But
look at those old-poem eyes staring at you from up (or down) the gentle
ring of light and darkness. Stare back and see them transform themselves in
the pleasure of your glance. They want to be understood, by you and nobody
else but you to the tune of a popular ditty. What they are saying is that
time is just another kind of space. And they are urging you to leap wildly
into seeing that free will doesn't ultimately exist. Begging you to take a
deterministic attitude towards the falling of the cosmic dice. Pleading with
you to absorb their hidden virtues and unexpected understandings of the you
that never was and always was. When you pay sufficient attention to the
radioactive eyes sprouting from the delicate and pathetic little petals
you've strewn along your path down through the tear-filled years you will
become worthy of remembering that you have written this poem as many times
as there are atoms in a puff of air. And that not a comma will be changed.
Or if you think you've changed a comma look again. Or why don't you just
give up and finish your whine, the ordinary domestic variety? But then again
sometimes all that is necessary is total familiarity with the manifold
operations of whatever it is we're talking about before you can be sure it
ain't really there. I'm not about to predict that you're about to become
another Nostradamus. But by the time you begin to become sickened by the
thought of eating the flesh of butchered animals you might with caution
predict that you're about to become a vegetarian. And all those jokes
you made about fur coats—and thought were funny! When we were kids
in the back seat of dad's car on the way to the lake we used to compete
to see who could see the lake first. I know what you're thinking, you're
thinking you can see the diamond, a subtle glow over the curve of this ring,
indisputably of great sentimental value but not entirely irreplaceable.
The eyes tell you that you know more than you think you know because
they know more than you know and they are your creations. And what
they know has nothing to do with you as you commonly define yourself.

90. How to Quit Smoking

I drop into Madame Bovary's for just one drink at five and at midnight
I'm still there, drinking until my hands start shaking, smoking until
blisters form on my tongue. Would it have anything to do with the fact
that the bartender, Felicity, reminds me a little of you? She flirts with all
the sad-eyed men but I think she flirts a little more with me. Tells me
I have a handsome nose, says she's interested in the occult. Every time
I go there she has her hair done up in a different way and so I don't
like to miss a day without at least peeking in to see how her hair is
and when I do I end up staying till closing time. I sit there at the bar
and my mind is blazing with brilliant and unutterable images of eternity.

She likes me because I'm no threat. Perhaps I'm a challenge. I catch her
eye staring thoughtfully at me from the side and she wants to know why
a relatively sane and attractive man like me doesn't have a mate. I tell her
it'd take me a year to explain but there is someone I deeply care for who
is currently (and probably forever) unavailable and all the others simply
aren't worth the trouble. "And that person reminds me a little of you,"
I say and she looks pleased. And so I begin to lie. "Same eyes," I say,
and she looks more pleased. "Same nose ... and, by golly, the same mouth.
Even your ears are similar." Meanwhile, Frank the farmer from Fergus,
Fred the famous (and recently divorced) photographer, and several other
horny men start wondering aloud why I'm getting all the attention.
It's because I'm not primarily interested in getting into her pants
I say and they say why not what's the matter with you? I'm a totally
asexual being, I say, rare as a unicorn and twice as precious. I'm a
poet, one who knows our existence as separate selves is an illusion,
so why should I want to fuck Felicity when I know we're all one anyway?
In the morning my mouth is so raw from all that smoking I place a fresh
package of Winston in my desk drawer and vow that whenever I feel the
urge to have one I'll remember what I said about our separate selves,
and that sticking silly things like cigarettes in one's mouth is simply
an expression of not seeing through the illusion of separate identities
(it's all a plot on the part of the mind that tries to sweet-talk the body
into thinking that smoking is somehow necessary, even good for it, so the
body will chainsmoke night and day until it withers up and dies and the
trapped but tyrannical mind, will, triumphant but tainted, finally fly free
and only then will it realize that demonologically there's nowhere to fly to),
and that we're all connected by rosy clouds of simple joy and desirelessness.

91. The Poetry of Our Age

When I read a poem about a poet sitting up all night by a pool of water
waiting for inspiration, the inspiration to write a pretty poem, that is,
rather than the inspiration to act, to find one's way out of difficulties,
out of grief or into grace, then I feel as if I could easily throw that poet
into that pool of water, there to drown. It is easy for someone today to name
three hundred widely acclaimed poets who write what they consider poetry
but which is impossible for a true poet to read because it is devoid of poetic
inspiration, not the kind that emerges from sweet nocturnal pools of water
but the kind that is everywhere for those with the depth of heart to see it.
All my poems now are not only dedicated but addressed to you, or should
I say my life is dedicated to you and my poems are addressed to you. And
through you and my love for you I am drowning in inspiration, crazed by
your absence and determined never to betray you. A poem that is exclusively
of academic interest is no poem, a poem must be of interest to everyone who
has experienced in the depths of his heart the wild passions of all our lives,
or it is no poem and the civilization that has produced it is no civilization.
Now and forever my life is dedicated to you and all the poems I have not yet
written will be addressed to you. Readers not yet born will search for hints
of your identity and some will perhaps conclude that you never existed
but were simply a goddess of my poor imagination, as if I spun myself a
little portable universe, one just large enough for the two of us to inhabit,
and we inhabit it only by virtue of our sense of the imaginary and divine.
Inspiration must be weeded out before it can flower. And I am drowning.
Drowning in a mind that is not large enough for my intelligence and a body
not strong enough for my love. There is not enough air in the atmosphere
for my puny lungs. Everywhere I look the universe is screaming at me.

The poets I know are like characters in novels, they've been driven insane
by their inability to remain under the waters of our common passion. They're
unable to read their own poems or the poems of anyone else with any degree
of felicity. We despise each other because we despise ourselves, we are all
little Irving Laytons who'd rather win the Nobel Prize than see peace in the
Middle East, see the world disarm, see poverty and starvation disappear.
We bear grudges and incredible jealousies because the stakes are so low.
We see brilliance in the work of our own hand, no matter how artificial
we know it to be, and nothing but confusion in the powerful work of the soul.
This is not our own sadness we feel, it's the sadness of the world which we
inflict upon ourselves because we are lost, afraid of death, afraid we are
already dead, and will go to any lengths to feel as if we belong on the earth.
Only certain people understand us, those who do can't explain us to others.
Our friends sense we're living corpses striving to be like everyone else.
Perhaps we noticed our friends were dead long before we noticed we were too.
The world is always full of peace and solemnity but only those incapable
of seeing themselves as anything other than dead are capable of noticing it.
Avoiding disturbing anyone's peace of mind is a full-time job. What are you
working on now? The enlightenment of all beings. When two people who know
each other simultaneously discover they are dead they immediately fall madly
in love. At least it seems that way to others. And in their dreams, which have
hitherto taken the form of a crystal eye hovering over their lives like the
clarity of eternity, they remember how sad they were as they stood on
opposite sides of the earth waving goodbye, then fading into a state of
sadness one imagines the ordinary summer clouds must feel: no sadness at all.
So we stared at each other across the distance, waved sadly, dissolved into
clouds (which, no matter how sad they may appear, are incapable of sadness).

92. A Date with Margaret Hollingsworth

Lately I've been going mad with inexplicable mysteries. People glance
nervously at me on the street and sense the blissful demons swarming
within my mild exterior, my eyes emitting mysterious coloured rays.
I walk past the Scientologists on Yonge Street and say to them no thanks,
I'm already perfectly clear, look at me, can't you see how clear I am?
They hold clipboards and ask me if I could be anywhere in the world where
would I want to be and I say right here, of course, that's why I'm here.
Usually they get mad but yesterday a black girl with a leaflet smiled.
I spend a lot of time thinking about simple things. Why, for instance,
a split second before the phone rings do you know it's going to ring?
There's a certain momentary absence of ringing, as if the phone had to
draw a quick breath before expelling its little electronic cry of alarm,
its infantile ding-a-ling plea to be picked up and cradled. And I wonder
why we're so miserable all the time in the midst of such an interesting
universe, why we're always getting in squabbles with the neighbours and
experiencing terrible emotional upheavals about lovers who don't love us
at least not the way we want to be loved and publishing little books of
poems which get hacked to death with the meat cleavers of other poets who
are blinded by jealousy and don't realize that if there's room enough for
all the people in the world surely there's room enough for all the poets
and writing poems about how we wish we could be as steadfast as a star
instead of simply being steadfast as a star or maybe even more steadfast.
I've vowed not to mention the nuclear arms race in any poem in which my
lovely (and talented) friend Margaret Hollingsworth appears. In the film
Yellow Earth the Chinese girl looks at the camera and says: Being single
is difficult but it's not as bad as being married. And my singular friend
Margaret Hollingsworth (who was there in the theatre with me) suddenly
yelled out: If thine eye be single then thy body will be full of light.
She'd been reading the Bible again, I guess. Boy, was I embarrassed.

The truth is I really wasn't embarrassed. I don't care about that sort of
thing any more. Not that I expect you to care really whether I care about
that sort of thing any more or not but no I shouldn't say that, I don't
mean to insult you or to downgrade the strength and purity of your love.
You loved me once, you will love me again, I know you love me now though
it's not possible owing to technical difficulties for you to pick up the
phone and tell me. Your continuing absence has given my poor old psyche
a strange loop that makes me glow faintly in the dark like a frigid planet
somewhere lost in a dark orbit around the abstract decimal point of a star
so distant it can't be seen, an orbit so long a moment is a year, a year
a millennium. I mean what are we? We are all tiny pimples of divine
consciousness on the skin of the world. All four billion of us. Maybe
five by the time you read this. Maybe six by the time I see you again.
Each of us as an individual is dead for all eternity, right? Except for a
brief flash of time in which we suddenly find ourselves alive. And
what do we do? We race around like mad, getting rich, making friends,
making love, making babies, making enemies, killing each other. Wouldn't
it make more sense just to sit still and enjoy life? Just enjoy the wild
peaceful bliss of being alive? Just sit still and shine like a star?
Sometimes I think our sacred duty as human beings is simply to sit still
and emit rays of ecstatic light in the immeasurably intelligent night.

93. The Lock on Basho's Gate

An afternoon wind arises and blows all my feelings away. I smile and
wave at them receding in the distance. How can this be? My heart's so
swollen and full of woe yet it's soaring high above the puffy clouds!
It's a miracle, though it's a pity to have to say so. On the telephone
you sigh and say what we have here is a classic case of melancholia
and I suggest that if only you could pay a visit all my dark angels
would fly away. Even though I know that when you left they'd fly back
and bring all their friends with them. And you mumble something about
not wanting to be responsible for such dramatic changes in my mood.
Sometimes it's such simple human dilemmas that make us realize we
aren't prepared for life or death. The dilemma of hearing on the telephone
the dear voice of a precious friend you'd happily try to swim Lake Ontario for
even though she is spending all her time with another man, spends each
night in his bed. Nothing in human history prepares us for these little
strangenesses. Such a darling voice. Full of the promise of timidly solemn
intimacy and heavenly felicity that is inexplicably never to be. Chaucer
was forever saying the bliss accompanying a marriage of true minds misses
the bliss of eternity by only half a point. But it's all so frightening,
and perhaps if it didn't frighten you then it would have to frighten me.
And there seems to be nothing I can do about the way my mind all by
itself just chats away to you for hours as I walk alone among the dead.

Basho has poems about weeping with loneliness in the middle of the night
yet he cherished his solitude and had to put a lock on his gate when his
fame as a poet brought him friends. For him, poetry was the way of solitude.
It started as an entertaining pastime but eventually became an obsession—
on his deathbed he was annoyed because he couldn't stop thinking about poems.
And Rilke was the Santa Claus of loneliness as Auden sarcastically called him
which perhaps makes me a Rilkian, a disciple, one of the North Pole elves.
All of whom keep their distance from each other. Last night, going to bed,
I was overcome with the cold weariness of the ages and thought I would like
to have put on my tombstone: He got up in the morning and went to his bed
at night over and over again until it drove him out of his mind. But then
I must have had a dream for everything is different today. It is unfair of me
to blame your absence for my angst. It's my absence from myself, not your
absence from me, my dislocation from that pivot around which the dreaded
days revolve, my inability to realize the wind that blows my feelings away
and causes my swollen heart to float above the clouds like the Goodyear blimp
is the same wind that flows in and out of my lungs, that inflames my aching
verse and engenders the miraculous love I bear. A human, love-bearing wind.

94. The Nosferatu Syndrome

If you know what you're doing you can do anything. Fate and faith or will
and desire have nothing to do with it. Everything is knowledge. Dying
is simply forgetting how to live. Impotence how to love. The pain
of being fully alive resurrects me like a Carmelite nun taking a vow
of martyrdom in an opera by Poulenc. I am old enough to remember when
telephone numbers had only five digits. Five-six-nine-four-eight, that
was ours when I was a kid, how can I ever forget it? I imagine engraved
on my tombstone: His phone number as a child was five-six-nine-four-eight.
No one had one like it. I had lunch with my brother today and he remembered
it too. Is this self-indulgence? One rainy evening in the forties, my dad
and I walking home from Kenilworth, and as we passed Crosthwaite he said:
"Wouldn't your mother be pleased if you had our phone number memorized by
the time we got home?" And I did and she was. It's like memorizing pain.
Being fully aware of all the pain you can be fully aware of is like being a
nun lulled by her simple understanding that everything is God, even the
beating of her little heart and the breathing of her little lungs, as she
sings her way along the catwalk to the guillotine at the end of act three,
her hands clasped in holiness, the mob shouting and jeering in demonic rage.

Caroline suggested we all drive up to Elora next weekend to visit her sister
and I said I had developed, in recent months, a phobia about being a
passenger in a car. And she pulled a huge tome from her shelf and searched
for a minute, then said: "Repressed grief." I feigned nonchalance but
felt a sudden foreign fingerprint deep in the virgin jungles of my heart.
I knew it was true! And for the next few days I had to face it: the world's
full of demons of my own creation, if I stop for a moment blazing with
perfect spiritual light they'll land on me and start sucking my blood,
and I'll have to admit my knowledge seems like nothing in your absence.

95. Christmas Eve at the Movies

I was standing in the Bathurst Subway Station on Christmas Eve and a
little Charlie Chaplin with holes in his shoes went up to the ticket
taker and said: "Let me in for free, will ya? I'm cold and broke."
The ticket taker looked both ways and said, "Okay go through quick."
I'd just been watching *Casablanca* and was simply dying for the chance
to use this line. I went up to the ticket taker, placed my arm on his
shoulder and said: "Ya did a good thing, boss." He looked both ways
again then looked at me and said: "Don't breathe a word to anyone,
I could get suspended for three days for this and with no pay."

Life imitates art but art imitates the noblest dreams when it's not
imitating other art. This morning my eyes slipped open with more than
normal sadness. All night I'd been dreaming we were together, and then
just before waking up I dreamt you had a baby, a perfect little girl,
and even though she'd just been born she kept hitting the keys and
yanking the paper as I tried to type. So I put my finger on her navel
and noticed her beauty which stopped my breath. "How did you get so
beautiful?" I murmured. She said, "I don't know." I almost fainted.
I sensed as she grew up she'd develop a taste for music and formalism,
and I figured all she'd need to become a poet would be the tendency
to have a lot to talk about and difficulty in finding people worth
talking to. The poet's special dilemma: the only ones willing to listen
are not the ones you particularly want to talk to. So you transform it
into the most mystical and minutely measured metres imaginable and summon
the faith to believe it'll be discovered by sympathetic hearts in faraway
lands with strange-sounding names and in unimaginable centuries to come.
Even those who wish their lives to imitate their noblest dreams find a
certain art is required. It's called magic. And when I die I want to see
William Shakespeare in radiant glory waiting there for me and I want him
to place his hand on my shoulder and say: "You did a good thing, boss."

96. Hummingbirds at Hell's Gate

Who do I think I am? I want my mind to have no bounds and sometimes it
feels as if it doesn't. This pathetic flickering light, so tiny, yet now and
then it feels it illuminates all of time and space, though not without many
immense shadows and much dullness. Last week, at Harrison Hot Springs,
still awake half an hour before dawn, cautiously opening the blinds, knowing
that horrible totem pole would be staring in at us, and behind it the lake and the
islands and the mountains looming above them, too dark to know how high,
and the tumultuous morning mist. I kept saying I was asleep and awake at the
same time, and you kept smiling to stop yourself from dozing off. Sometimes
laughing wildly at my little jokes. It was like we were floating. I used to think
the hardest thing about writing was maintaining the belief that it mattered. But
now somehow I feel my powers are immense, I transform the world, and you.
I used to write for everyone, now I write for you, an unadulterated blend of
solemnity and rapture which at times I imagine Mozart might have noticed.

I flew back to Toronto sitting next to a Roman Catholic nun (none better!)
who kept enthusing about the unity of all of life, the non-multiplicity
of the universe. Did you tell her that was pure Buddhism, you said, and I
said I didn't get a chance, she told me that. And I know it's true but still
I miss you today, a sudden feeling of lusty emptiness that started last
night and is going to continue at least until I fall asleep tonight. There
was really nothing spectacular about our little trip by rented car up the
Fraser Canyon: I was dull, you were dull, even the heroic scenery was dull
(we agreed we prefer a natural beauty less whorishly obvious and democratic).
Now I miss that dullness, Eden's splendid dullness before the fall, when
being is everything, being fused, being together full of immensities unknown,
when everything outside of ourselves is merely a dimly pleasant and harmless
little distraction, and maybe this dullness has something to do with the
special metaphysical task life sends our way: to bring to consciousness
the knowledge that was ours before the birth of consciousness. Like being
awake and asleep at the same time. The guy at the Hell's Gate Airtram,
he said he was from St. Catharines, I gave him my Giant Panda pin for his
collection, he reminded you of me. And all those Chinese labourers who died
blasting rock for the tracks to come through, and Simon Fraser, and over
it all we went, with a special kind of boredom that didn't mean we weren't
perfectly happy to be there, soaring over the Fraser Canyon in a tiny box.
And so in spite of the boredom we admit we have a certain weight between us
that makes us glad we've found one another and we know we'd never be able
to lose one another, not totally, though talk like this is almost a crime,
because we leave unsaid all the horrors of our modern age. The arts of peace
and all the willed blindness they demand. Every day and night we've spent
together seem like yesterday and last night. The clock turns to butter and
runs down the wall whenever we exchange glances. The sun and moon turn
into brimming pails of artificial nectar. We sat in the little tourist restaurant
overlooking the canyon and ate chunks of fresh salmon and watched the
hummingbirds sipping artificial nectar. You asked if they went south in the
winter and I said no they hibernate like little humming bears, in tiny caves in
the limestone cliffs, sleeping in perfect little humming circles, an inch off the
ground, never dreaming of their own imminent extinction, just dreaming. Later
we found out they migrate with the spring, following the blossoms up from
sunny Ecuador, but their little humming compasses get jammed when people
put out those nectar dispensers, with callous disregard for their northern neighbours.

97. The Women in My Life

I love life, it's just that I don't like my own life very much. I'm
trapped everywhere I turn, bound wrist and ankle by my own mind-forged
mandibles. But life itself, don't get me wrong, I think it's basically
a good idea. I mean I'm so smart I'm stupid. I can't make up my mind
about anything. I see both sides of every argument, and so my argument
with myself can never be won, will have to drone on till the very end
of everything, never mind my argument with you in which both of us take
both sides. They say Jesus will save you if you ask sincerely enough
even if you're not a Christian. So for Christ's sake, Jesus, save me,
I have been mistakenly buried alive. I know I have only a gulp of breath
left, with folded hands I beseech you to let me enter your holy presence.

It's the women in my life. Sonja, who knows nothing about it, reads my
poems with bloody-minded intensity and asks pointed questions about my
divorce. She says what most men did in their twenties I'm doing in my
how old are you again? I say if only it were that simple! She knows or
thinks she knows about Betsy the Typesetter (she introduced us), who is now
living in Seattle with Bob and baby Waldo. She doesn't know about Janet
who says I'm good-looking for a white man and I have such dangerous dancing
eyes and I dress with flair and move beautifully but I'm too hung up on work
and age (she's eighteen years younger), she says she wants to drown me with
exotic colour, she wants to fall hopelessly in love with me and then when I
reject her she wants to dress up all in black in front of the mirror and blow her
brains out. She doesn't know about Annie who just got back from Paris with
Tim and seems blissfully unconcerned that it wasn't with me. And then there's
Leslie whom Janet saw me walking down Yonge Street with a couple of weeks ago,
eating ice cream and laughing merrily, which of course renewed her interest in me.
The spirit of the world is sweet and tender, it billows endlessly, creating life, and never
makes a mistake or thinks a thought. And then there's Celine, oh what a night
in Lighthouse Park with the towering firs and cedars and the full moon like
a divine spotlight casting us as Adam and Eve on the stage of our innocence.
And then there's you, my instincts say don't tell you about all these things
but if I don't you'll call me a liar when you otherwise find out. Last night
I tried to teach Janet a little about poker because all her friends have been
playing strip poker lately and she always ends up first to be naked. And
although everybody talks about the metaphysics of baseball it suddenly
occurred to me what is poker if not a simple ritual for creating order
out of chaos, with a pot of gold going to the hero who does it best, with
raw skill not being as favoured as much as the skill of being able to
recognize the elements of order in the chaos being dealt you at random
every moment. Is this what Christ meant when he said he who hates his life
will find it? Shall I go truly mad? Christ was nailed to the cross as our
Christ-like spirits are nailed to our hands and feet, our tiny inadequate brains
and our little eyes that seldom get a rest from tears, from unrealistic desires.
How long will I be able to bear the dilemmas of my life, the dilemmas that
drive me into dangerous solitary brooding about the insanely convoluted path
my spirit seems intent on leading me, the horrendous burdens it gives me,
burdens I could quite frankly very easily place down and forget but won't?
And how much happier would I be surrounded by famine, pestilence and war?
I've always been this way but only lately have I begun to notice it
and now that I can see it so clearly I know I'm not going to be able
to bear it much longer, I know I'm going to have to burst my chains and
quit mixing metaphors and when I do will the shock drive me insane or
will it precipitate a great spiritual awakening, an entry to a new world?

98. A Home Run Is a Glorious Thing

On my way to the streetcar I passed a little softball game and the batter
got a home run just as I passed so I knew it was a good omen and the Jays
would win and they did, beat first-place Boston 5-1, the Jays something like
twelve games behind Boston and it's only June. My first baseball poem and
already I sound like watered-down Raymond Souster or even Kenny Norris on a
particularly sentimental day. Exhibition Stadium, a night game, Lake Ontario
gulls waddling around in the outfield, Lloyd Moseby got a homer (his ninth)
and so did Jesse Barfield (his fifteenth) and one of the college kids a row
behind sighed and said "A home run is a glorious thing." I turned and smiled
dreamily and he smiled back. They'd been talking softly about Brenda Vaccaro.
And it's true a homer in the park is much more interesting than one on TV.
The sun went down and a little crescent moon came out in the west, the evening
star gleaming, the sky going through shades of green and gold as it darkened.
Already I'm an expert, already I know the Jays have a good chance at Boston,
and already I know it doesn't matter because win or lose they're fun to watch
and you get the feeling they can win whenever they put their No Mind to it.

There was nobody hollering vicious insults at the players, a polite but huge
Canadian crowd still new to big-league ball, and when the batter had to duck
a wild pitch an old guy down from me sitting next to a guy with a portable
radio said, quietly: "Geez, what're you trying to do, hit the guy?" Again
I turned and smiled dreamily and the guy smiled back. There was Malcolm Gray
and his lovely wife and their small son in a Blue Jays cap and the boy's nanny
(who had white skin and black hair and three silver rings in her left ear)
and I sneaked up behind Malcolm (who had binoculars and a portable radio) and
whispered in his ear we should wear our silver helmets to these games (helmets
presented by the Hamilton Fire Department in 1974 to Gray and McFadden for
distinguished spot-news reporting, in which no firefighters were embarrassed)
and he turned and said yeah we should have, you still got yours? And I said no
I lost it when I lost my sanity one day and found my soul which, it turns out,
strangely resembles the CNE Stadium full of people and ballplayers and gulls
on a warm night in early June in the second half of my life when you discover
the only wisdom worth having, the wisdom that comes with knowing the only
wisdom worth anything is the wisdom that comes with knowing the only wisdom,
and so on, and I think for a moment of the nature of our love, yours and mine,
and I wonder if say I got cancer and withered away in a matter of weeks, I
imagine myself on my death bed, the nurse coming in with a phone and helping
me sit up to say hello. You'd say I'm just calling to say hi, do you have a
minute, then you'd chat merrily for a few minutes, then you'd say well I
have to go now, can I give you a little call in a few days? So then I thought
maybe I'm getting bored with the long wait for you to make up your mind
about me and maybe I'm getting interested in baseball because you're not.
(Later I decide to leave these last nine lines in despite their silliness,
you can't delete an inning just because of embarrassing play, right? In fact
the most embarrassing plays are the most interesting and always get shown
on the evening news. The entire game, in all its details, is intact forever.)

99. Proust

In the past few days I've become inexplicably super-aware of the vast and
endless symphony that goes on all around us all the time. It's the last day
of September and the schoolbells and traffic guard's whistles and sentimental
sounds of children playing, babies crying, fills me with the kind of joy I've
hitherto associated with listening to Beethoven quartets. Yesterday I became
entranced with the magic and endlessly varying sound of the subway and when
we reached the Davisville station an energetic young Doberman pinscher was
galloping up and down the platform and I wished it would bark but alas it
didn't. Suddenly I love dogs, and mainly for their unpredictable barking, and
so often the bark of a dog will come at exactly the right moment and pitch.
The dog's bark is as essential to it as the tree's and somehow it has become
essential to me as well, although I realize such barking can be overdone,
particularly late at night. I was talking to my mother the other day by the
way and she said the only time she can ever remember seeing me in a completely
happy mood was when she saw me with you. Well, she didn't actually come out
and say it in so many words but that's the intention she wished to convey.

And yesterday I broke down and bought the Kilmartin/Moncrieff Proust in three
volumes. Remember that phony Hungarian poet Carlos San Domingo used to say:
"La recherche du temps perdu, it just can't be said in English"; and I'd
say: "What? It's a translation, from Shakespeare's English, you dumb nut.
When to the sessions of sweet silent thought." And he'd quickly change the
subject, to something else he didn't know anything about. And on the subway
coming home I met a beautiful intelligent charming sexy Frenchwoman who was
reading (and you're going to have trouble believing this) Proust. She liked me
too and when our eyes met she took off her sweater (it was warm) and stole
more intimate glances at me standing over her. I showed her my new-bought
volumes and she became quite friendly. I told her for years I vowed never to
read Proust until I was able to read him in French but alas it was still not
possible and I have finally acknowledged it will never be. And she said Proust
is difficult even for the French and perhaps I should be reading, in French,
Balzac, who writes in sentences of a more sensible length. And then I said
oh it's my stop and ran off, sensing a definite disappointment in her face,
and I wondered about that, wondered if perhaps I should have given her my
card, or gone on a few more stops with her, walked her home perhaps, she was
truly a fine woman and I'm sure we had the potential for a warm friendship,
but I went home, realizing we would never meet again in the sad city, and
after slowly reading the entire "Overture," alone in my apartment late last
night, I became renewed in my appreciation of the incredible richness and
peacefulness of my solitude, full of books, contemplation, freedom and peace.
And, so warmly fulfilling it stuns me to think of it, my distant love for you.

100. Dead Hippopotamus

You're right: my poems are seldom as quiet as they could be. I want them
flower-like and full of equilibrium, their power deeply buried. Quietly
reflecting the quiet and unregarded miracles occurring all around them.
They should never worry about being noticed among all the other poems.
If they are truly and sincerely blossom-like and in addition technically well
constructed it would be impossible for them to envy the poems of others.
And so I slept poorly after our visit last night and in the morning I went out
for a paper and coffee and there at the corner of Parliament and Carlton
was a dead hippopotamus. It had been in a collision with two cars and was
lying there, its eyes already sunken and dry with death, its thick flesh
dull and dusty. It looked stupid lying there, a beast never to roam again.
In a land in which such beasts are not native, are kept locked up in zoos,
it reminded me of the long-delayed death of exotic but ridiculous dreams.

When I was a cowboy in Alberta once we found a calf wandering half-starved
and it was obvious the mother had died. And so we rode out looking for her.
She'd crawled into a small wooden shed and died there and in the summer heat
her carcass had bloated until it filled the entire shed and it kept bloating
until the shed had slowly exploded from the internal pressure. And the horrid
flyblown stench under the blue sky and white clouds of the endless prairie,
far from roads. Like these grossly bloated sonnets, bursting through the
shed of common poetic decency. As for the hippo, there was no stench,
no bloating, just a dry rot from within, a terrible dryness and lack of life.
And it looked as if it had been dead centuries, drowned in an African bog,
then discovered and placed at a busy intersection to advertise traffic safety.
Well, the things you said last night, there is nothing I want to do. We had
the occasional taste of bliss together over the years and my or was it our
fantasy that some day we'd be free to be together and experience that bliss
constantly was the psychological equivalent of a big stupid hippo covered
with birds and flies and drinking swamp water tainted with assorted poisons.
"I think I need your poems more than your poems need me, and I'm not just
saying that to be polite," you said. But you also said you found them often
too attentive, too clever, and they tended to dominate you in a way that was
sometimes exhausting, sometimes frightening, sometimes demonic. Your criticism
I accept easily, in fact I probably knew all along the poems were all wrong,
they tried to accomplish certain things, they even tried to manipulate your
emotions, they flexed their biceps on beaches, they posed in front of mirrors,
they were irresponsible, tried to tell you things that perhaps were not true.
This represents another in a long line of betrayals of the spirit of poetry.
Poems are not meant to persuade, exhaust, frighten, they are not meant to
say what cannot be said with a quiet glance, and one should not write so
many of them that they are in danger of being in collision with dumb animals.

Acknowledgements

"The CN Tower" and "Hell" previously appeared in *Rampike*, "My Grandmother Learns to Drive" in *The Montreal Journal of Poetics*, "Windsurfers," "My Own True Nature," "Nipples" (under the title "Angels and Lovers"), "The Robe of Your Intelligence," "Conversation with a Small Herd of Cattle" and "The Two of Cups" in *Descant*, "How to Be Your Own Butcher" in *Canadian Literature* (twice!), "Beer and Pizza" in *Zest*, "Heading towards Buchenvald," "Monkey on My Back," "Jellyfish of Light," "Consciousness," "Elephants on Television," "Love's Like Milk," "A Visit to the Zoo," "Elephants," "Shantideva," "The Inchworm," "Terrible Storm on Lake Erie" and "Blue Irises" in *The Malahat Review*, "How to Quit Smoking" in *The Canadian Forum*, and "A Home Run Is a Glorious Thing" in *Innings*. "The Poetry of Our Age" was published in April 1986 as a broadsheet by Nicky Drumbolis of Letters Books in his "2 Bit Poetry" series. Public readings of these poems have been given at Kent Penitentiary in Kent, British Columbia, the Western Front in Vancouver, the Hornby Island Poetry Institute on Hornby Island, British Columbia, the Canadian Forum Cabaret at the Bamboo Club in Toronto, Letters Books in Toronto, the University of Canterbury in Christchurch, New Zealand, Victoria University in Wellington, New Zealand, Massey University in Palmerston North, New Zealand, the University of Auckland in Auckland, New Zealand, the Australian National University in Canberra, Australia, and, in a collaborative performance entitled "The Writer and the Gypsy Cleaning Lady" with dancer/singer/actress/writer Margaret Dragu, at various public libraries in small towns in Southern Ontario during the National Book Festival of 1987. In addition I'd like to acknowledge the various kinds of moral and inspirational assistance issuing from individuals connected with the following authorities, alliances, affiliations and associations: The Public Lending Right Commission, the Writer's Union of Canada, the Canada Council, the Canadian Department of External Affairs, the Ontario Arts Council, the Coincidence Club, the Ontario Ministry of Community and Social Services, the University of Western Ontario, the Metropolitan Toronto Public Library, the Hamilton Public Library, Talon Books, Firefly Books, Black Moss Press, Coach House Press, the Marcel Proust Bowling, Roller Skating and Great Books Club, the Association of Gentlemen of Sensible Height, and the Toronto Blue Jays. And a tip of the hat to the fans. Direct all correspondence to David W. McFadden, c/o the Hugh Garner Co-op, 550 Ontario Street, Toronto M4X 1X3.